WALK ONE HOUR

I dedicate this book
to the people of the Parish of St Francis of Assisi,
Long Eaton, Derbyshire,
who were the first to put these pages to the test.

JOSEPH O'HANLON

Walk One Hour

Stations of the Cross
for Pilgrim People

ST PAULS

Quotations from Scripture are from a number of excellent modern translations and many are my own translations. I have tried to use the translation which most tellingly contributed to the meditative and prayerful intent of each Station. I hereby acknowledge use within the permitted limits of the following:

Revised Standard Version of the Bible, copyright 1946, 1952, 1971, and 1973 by the Division of Christian Education of the National Council of the Churches of Christ in the United States of America.
New Revised Standard Version of the Bible, copyright 1989 and 1995 by the Division of Christian Education of the National Council of the Churches of Christ in the United States of America.
The New Jerusalem Bible, copyright 1985 by Darton, Longman and Todd, London.
New American Bible, copyright 1999 by the Zondervan Corporation, Grand Rapids, Michigan 49530.

ST PAULS Publishing
187 Battersea Bridge Road, London SW11 3AS, UK
www.stpauls.ie

ISBN 085439 695 0

Set by Tukan DTP, Fareham, UK
Printed by Interprint Ltd., Marsa, Malta

ST PAULS is an activity of the priests and brothers
of the Society of St Paul who proclaim the Gospel
through the media of social communication

Contents

That I did always love
I bring thee Proof
That till I loved
I never lived — Enough —

That I shall love always —
I argue thee
That love is life —
And life hath Immortality —

This — dost thou doubt — Sweet —
Then have I
Nothing to show
But Calvary —

                    Emily Dickinson

Preface

There is a time to live and a time to die. Christian faith is founded on belief in a benign God and, all the more strangely, on the death, by divine decree, of the very one revered as God's Son. The contradiction inherent in a faith that adheres to a God of living beings – creator, sustainer, destiny – and a faith which proclaims a death in its central act of worship, needs, if it is to be a faith which enlightens the human mind, study, reflection, and prayer. Mary's instinct was to ponder these things in her heart, an instinct which issued, but only after careful scrutiny, in a willing assent of the mind, and in a glorious outpouring of prayer (the *Magnificat*). Such wisdom from one who knew the heart of the matter should not be passed over lightly.

Walk One Hour seeks to listen to the words of Mary, take them to heart, and pray them as the Spirit moves. To stand with Mary at the foot of the Cross is to be in the right place, the only place, to hear the word of God clearly and unambiguously, and to be empowered to keep it, to cleave to it as the very stuff of life. To stand at the Cross is to resolve the paradox that out of this death living becomes possible. No other place reveals this secret. This little book seeks no more than to help people to make their way to Calvary, to encourage them to remain there awhile, and to leave the rest to God.

My reflections on the death of Jesus over many years have been enriched by my students, by my friends, and a host of writers whose wisdom is evident on every page of this book. To all these I am thankful. I am especially indebted to three students whose pastoral

7

insights were a sure guide. They undertook to read my manuscript with the appropriately jaundiced eye of the hard-pressed and dedicated parishioner. To Laura Parris, Pauline Green, and Graham Wheater, I acknowledge a great debt and offer my heartfelt thanks.

The illustrations accompanying the text are a reproduction in black and white of The Way of the Cross, painted by Vincent Wells, MBE, and which adorn the Church of Mary Immaculate, Grantham, Lincolnshire. Their inclusion in this book is, I hope, a tribute to a dear friend to whom I owe more than words can say. It is no small thing to guide a bewildered, newly ordained curate into good sense, especially with kindness, wisdom, and great good humour. To the parishioners of Grantham who received me with such kindness, I wish to say, with St Paul, that I remember you constantly and with deep affection before the Lord.

Walk One Hour

We spend too little time at the foot of the Cross. The Cross is our sign but it is more often around our necks than in our minds and hearts. Of course it is more comfortable, more reassuring, to stand at the empty tomb, looking up to heaven, our thoughts on eternity and bliss to come. But we must ponder one indelible truth: Christ is risen – we are not.

The death of Jesus is surely the most consequential in history. Whether one is a Christian, whether one has ever heard of Jesus or not, it is impossible to write him out of history. Wars have been waged in his name, the greatest works of art have been inspired by his life and death, saints and sinners have sought refuge under his wing.

Yet Christians have a reluctance to sit upon the ground at the foot of the Cross to think and pray, to ponder, and pray again. There was a time when many "did the Stations" during Lent but those days of fasting and fish have gone and we are the worse for it. For all of these penances, these irritations, were close to the pain of life; they reminded us of human pain, of human weakness, of our need to be with the world of destitution. When we were all poorer, we prayed the Passion of Jesus more often and with an unspoken, unremembered conviction that we would be close to God if we were close to the Cross. The more secure we have become in our western world of wealth, the more we have abandoned reminders of our mortality, our Lenten prayers and penances, which confronted us with the death of Jesus and so with our own. The more comfortable we have become, the more we have "forsaken him and fled" (Mark 14:50). What is proposed in these pages is a return to Calvary, to the Place of the Skull, in order to allow His death to speak again to our minds and hearts, to rehabilitate our symbols and make the Sign of the Cross speak to our time and our place.

We need to remember things past. The connection between what happened (what *really* happened) on that first Good Friday and what has happened, and continues to happen, to our faith in God, has been broken. We see our Church disintegrating all around us. We see our families and schools turning out young adults who wish to have little or nothing to do with much that their parents and grandparents held sacred and strengthening and essential to their very well-being. We have witnessed the destruction of our culture by forces we little understand but whose effects have all but wiped out our way of living and dying.

We need to dig and delve around the roots. We need to leave aside inessential things, and to return to the bedrock of our faith, and begin to "re-fresh" our minds and our spirits, and, indeed, our bodies. Walking the way to Calvary is a metaphor for walking our way to life. Each step of the way confronts us with the realities of our lives by holding them up to the mirror of His life. What has brought catastrophe to our Churches is our refusal to remember the birth pains which brought us into being in the first place. We were born at the Place of the Skull, not out of the empty womb of the tomb. It was the suffering and death of Jesus which brought us to life: *by his wounds we are healed* (Isaiah 53:5). Resurrection is the confirmation of God's commitment to humanity; crucifixion is the thing itself.

10

The Stations of the Cross

The Stations of the Cross is an ancient prayer, an old remembrance of the death of Jesus. The very first accounts of the death of Jesus were told by story-tellers whose lives had been devastated by the horrific agony of a crucifixion but miraculously transformed by the hand of God. Death was not the end of the story but, to understand what lay beyond the death, it was necessary to retrace the steps which led to the Place of the Skull, to Golgotha, the old quarry where the mortal life of Jesus was so brutally ended. And the going back, the retracing of the steps, was always a prayer, a meditation, an argument with God (the essence of prayer) as to the whys and the wherefores. The first disciples of Jesus who sought to make their way back to Calvary were not seeking merely to understand what happened to Jesus but to discover what happened to themselves, to learn (again and again), not only what God had set out to do in the life of Jesus but what he determined to realise in their lives. To go again to Golgotha was not simply to discover who Jesus was. It was to discover themselves.

The journey, therefore, was a prayer. It was a struggle to find the hand of God in all the pain and suffering. Prayer opens up new possibilities, proposes new challenges, offers new opportunities. Prayer is dangerous because it demands change. To walk to Calvary in prayer is to court the hazard of conversion, the risk of upheaval, the heartache of rebuilding. Going to the place of the death of Jesus is a Lenten experience; it will call for listening, learning, leaning and limping. Listening, because we are transfigured by listening (Mark 9:2-8). Learning, because the Christian must know what went on there and why. Leaning, because it is a hard place and we have to lean on ourselves to take in what we learn there and live by it. Everyone who goes to the Cross and learns what it means, comes away with a limp. Wrestling with God is always hazardous and always leaves scars. Ask Jacob who wrestled with God and came away limping (Genesis 32:22-32). And to these, add loving because *God so loved the world*... But we only know it is love we have found when we make our way there and sit upon the ground.

A Brief History

The crucifixion of Jesus was a matter of routine. The imperial might of Rome used crucifixion as a deliberate act of terror. Runaway slaves, bandits, robbers, thieves, would-be revolutionaries and rebels, anyone, indeed, who threatened or appeared to threaten imperial power, was crucified. Crucifixion was always a public act, as much a dire warning to onlookers as punishment for malefactors. And it was a routine, everyday occurrence, in every conquered city and town from York to Jerusalem. The Jewish historian Josephus, a near contemporary of St Mark, relates that two thousand people were crucified in Jerusalem following disturbances after the death of Herod the Great in 4 BC and that five hundred people a day were crucified outside the city after the destruction of the Temple in 70 AD. By all appearances, the death of Jesus was so far from exceptional that one wonders why a crowd is said to have gathered for the occasion.

The tiny group of frightened followers of Jesus had little reason to venerate the Place of the Skull, as Mark named it. It was difficult enough to try to explain that a crucified criminal embodied the will of God for humanity's future without turning the site of the tragedy into a shrine. Then the sad fact is that the Christian child moved away from its Jewish parent. The disastrous Jewish uprisings against imperial Rome (66-73 AD and again, 132-135 AD), and the increasingly daring directions of Christian thought, caused Jewish parent and Christian child to go their separate ways and, disastrously, to generate the kind of bitterness endemic in family estrangements. As Christianity made its way in the pagan world, there was little desire to remember where it began, on a crucifixion hill, with the death of a Jewish criminal, outside the Jewish city of Jerusalem, in the shadow of the Jewish Temple where God dwelt on earth.

The city of Jerusalem, razed to the ground during two hopeless attempts to shake off the yoke of Rome, was rebuilt after 135 AD by the emperor Hadrian and named Aelia Capitolina. Jews were forbidden to live there and a temple in honour of the goddess Aphrodite adorned the place where God's Temple had stood. Where Jesus died, Aphrodite reigned.

After the Council of Nicaea in 325 AD, the first Christian emperor, Constantine, with no little encouragement from his mother, decreed that the site should be cleared and the great Basilica of the Holy Sepulchre be built where Jesus had been buried and raised again to new life. What is surprising is that this great church was not (and is not) called the Basilica of the Holy Resurrection. The instinct of true pilgrims is to stand at the foot of the Cross before over-hastily running to the empty tomb.

Pilgrims began to trace the steps of Jesus, or what they thought were the steps of Jesus on that fateful day in Jerusalem. We have a fifth century account by a Spanish nun, Egeria, and pilgrimages continued throughout the Middle Ages, although Muslim dominance in Jerusalem and throughout the Middle East inhibited access by Christian pilgrims.

Popular devotion to Christ's passion in the eleventh century led to pictorial representations of the last events of Christ's life in such great Gothic churches as those at Rheims, Amiens and Chartres. The Crusaders, with their emblem of the Cross of Christ (hence the name, from *crux*, meaning "cross") and their exploits in the Holy Land (a dismal chapter in Christian history), encouraged devotion to the Cross. Although the practice of building churches and chapels in which the events of Christ's life were remembered goes back at least to the fourth century in Jerusalem, it was not until the fifteenth century that such "stations" became common-place in Europe and were used, together with devotional booklets, after the invention of printing, to assist the stay-at-home pilgrim to participate in the Way of the Cross.

Famous freestanding Stations of the Cross were set up as miniature chapels by the Dominican friar Alvarez in the monastery of Scala Coeli near Cordoba. The relief stations of the "Seven Falls of Christ" (1490/1505) by Adam Krafft in Nuremberg and the Calvary of Varallo are justly famous. By the fourteenth century, the Franciscans had instituted the Holy Circulus in Jerusalem, a devotional procession from site to site. The English pilgrim William Wey was the first to describe each stop on the way as a "station" (1458/1462).

In the late Middle Ages, the number of stations varied greatly, from seven in the German-speaking lands to as many as forty-three elsewhere. The process by which we arrived at the fourteen stations known today began in the late sixteenth century and in 1731 Pope Clement XII fixed the number at fourteen. Nine of the fourteen stations reflect incidents recorded in the Gospels and five from other strands of tradition. The mediations and prayers which accompany the Stations of the Cross are many and varied. Most Catholics are familiar with those of St Alphonsus Ligouri.

The Way to Golgotha
according to St Mark

St Paul's letters to Christian communities are the first writings which have come down from the very earliest followers of Jesus. Of course, those who followed Jesus to Jerusalem and were participants in the tragedy which occurred there, were the first to tell the story and to relate it to others in order to convince them of God's hand in what had been done there. From the very beginning, in other words, the story was preached, that is, it was told in order to win people to a new understanding of life and its possibilities.

St Paul never met Jesus and he provides us with very few details of the life of Jesus. Yet, throughout his letters to Christian communities, scarcely a page fails to mention the death of Jesus. Indeed, he states quite emphatically that *we preach Christ crucified* (1 Corinthians 1:23) and, just a few lines further on, *I know nothing among you except Jesus Christ and him crucified* (1 Corinthians 2:2). Paul realised that, from a human point of view, to do so was stuff and nonsense (1 Corinthians 1:23) but, from God's perspective, it was wisdom beyond all telling. And, stranger still, Paul, in line with all early Christians, chose an obscure and surprising word to describe his message concerning the meaning of the death of Jesus: he called it "gospel", "good news", indeed, "the gospel of God" (Romans 1:1). For Paul "the good news of God" meant two things. It was, of course, good news *from* God. But, more tellingly, it was good news *about* God. The Stations of the Cross is a prayerful, meditative attempt to discover what the suffering and death of an obscure Jew has to say about God. The Way of the Cross is no more and no less than a journey into the very heart of God.

Paul became a Christian three or four years after the death of Jesus. Those who had travelled to Jerusalem with Jesus, and were there at the death, were still alive and telling the story and explaining its meaning. It was never enough to relate what happened. What happened needed to be interpreted. What did it mean? Where was the hand of God in this gruesome tragedy? What does it mean? What does it mean to me? These were the questions which surrounded the death of Jesus from that dismal Friday afternoon, and which the likes of Peter and Andrew, James and John, Mary, Joanna, and Salome, had to answer, if they were to win people to their way of thinking about God and what God had done.

Time went on and the story was told beyond the confines of Jerusalem and Palestine, each new time, each new place requiring explanation and interpretation. How can a criminal's death be God's good news to men and women? The first tellers and interpreters began to die and the gospel came to be written down. Thus gospel which was told became a *Gospel* which was written.

Many *Gospels* came to be written but four of them, Matthew, Mark, Luke and John, came to occupy a particular place in Christian tradition as cornerstones of faith. These *Gospels*, along with other writings of the earliest Christians, came to form the New Testament, the foundational documents of what we believe and how we live.

To the best of our knowledge, Mark was the first to write the story of the death of Jesus, the first who decided that the events leading to the death of Jesus could be committed to writing in such a way as to bring out the significance of what happened at Golgotha. We know very little about Mark and even the earliest traditions concerning him do not provide the kind of hard evidence which might be fashioned into a dependable biography. However, we may say with a great degree of certainty that Mark was a companion of St Peter who wrote his *Gospel* in Rome in the aftermath of the killing, by crucifixion and other heinous means, of many Christians who had been falsely condemned by Emperor Nero (54–68 AD) for burning the imperial capital city (July, 64 AD). Mark wrote to rehabilitate the shattered Christian community and he did so by recounting in his little book some of the events which led to the crucifixion of Jesus. He attempted to link the fate of Jesus with the fate of the beleaguered Christians, to interpret the death of Jesus in Jerusalem so that it made some sense of the catastrophe which had befallen his followers in Rome. Mark did not simply tell the story; that would never be enough. In the telling he had to translate its significance from the quarry in Jerusalem to the streets of Rome. He had so to present the story of the death of Jesus that it spoke anew to his time and his place. He was turning history into gospel. His first line reads, *Beginning the gospel of Jesus Messiah, Son of God* (Mark 1:1).

Mark's Gospel was once described as the Passion of Jesus with a long introduction. But, in truth, from beginning to end, it is entirely concerned with the death of Jesus. The challenge which his little book throws out to Christian hearers and readers is to turn his Gospel into good news for our time and our place, to do for our time and our place what he did for his. This requires the discipline of prayer, the solitude of reflection, and the determination of conversion. To undertake the Way of the Cross with St Mark is to risk discipleship.

Preparing to Walk One Hour...

Walk One Hour is intended to be versatile. These explanatory notes and suggestions are no more than that and it is to be hoped that these pages will stimulate imagination and creativity rather than encourage slavish adherence. When it comes to understanding the Gospels and especially the death of Jesus, imagination is the best of guides, provided it is schooled by the disciplines of study, reflection, and prayer.

GENERAL REMARKS

Walk One Hour is intended to be a four-year programme. Each station begins with the discipline of study, then reflection, then prayer. We begin with the passion and death of Jesus as recorded in the first Gospel to be written: that according to St Mark. We will, God willing, continue the journey through the passion stories of Matthew, Luke and John.

The enterprise, let me repeat, involves study, reflection and prayer. The Background introductions to each step of the Way, to each station, may be studied privately, in family, neighbourhood or parish groups. But they are essential: study there must be. Otherwise, reflection and prayer will be sterile. And it is to be hoped that study will stimulate argument and debate, for these too, are part of prayer.

The purpose of this exercise of the heart and mind must be clearly grasped. It is to achieve an understanding of the death of Jesus of Nazareth. To understand the death of Jesus is, as St Paul constantly reminds us, to understand the gospel of God. "We preach Christ crucified" (1 Corinthians 1:23) is his constant slogan. He knew that to begin to penetrate the mystery of the Cross was to begin to penetrate the heart of God. If we are to understand what God is about in our world, what the Church is for, and why our witness is demanded, then we will learn at the foot of the Cross and nowhere else.

While it is possible to *Walk One Hour* as a personal journey, it is intended to be a community experience. Church is the best place and there is the added penance of having to get there. While most Catholic churches and chapels have Stations of the Cross, for the purposes of this journey to Calvary it would be better to make a large, plain wooden cross, with no figure. It would be more in keeping with historical accuracy to fashion a T, rather than a +. During Lent, the cross should be set in a prominent place, easy of access and plain to view by all who frequent the church. It should be shrouded with a purple veil, to be removed at the beginning and replaced at the end of each station with appropriate solemnity. The permanent unveiling on Good Friday should be the culmination of the journey, which has revealed some of the true meaning of what happened at the Place of the Skull. Imagination is called for if dramatic effect is to be realised.

Each station may be led by a priest, deacon or lay person from any community of Christians. It may be led by a man or a woman. Whoever the leader, leadership should be undertaken only by those committed to careful preparation. A group should be formed to prepare painstakingly for each station. Setting, adornment, music, readings, reflections, prayers – all need to be subjected to discussion and planning. It may be that different groups will be given responsibility of one or more stations and, accordingly, there needs to be a leader with oversight of the whole enterprise, a leader who knows how to animate people, to identify talent and to encourage its service for the good of all. A family group, a school group, a parish group, all as representative and as ecumenical as possible, could be entrusted with the presentation of each station. The aim should be to delegate responsibility to those who will best exercise it and to provide advice and encouragement for those who accept what is an onerous task. Accepting burdens for the good of all is, of course, a little crucifixion. But, then, that is the whole point.

MUSIC

Competent people should undertake to oversee the music, which is an essential element of *Walk One Hour*. I have made suggestions but I have no competence in this area and my prejudices are evident in what I have proposed. Ancient prayers (*Kyrie, Agnus Dei, Stabat Mater, Ubi Caritas*), familiar chants from Taizé, hymns ancient and modern, Bach, Beethoven, Blues and Beatles – all may serve as prayer and all may mark the journey to Calvary.

READINGS

Readings are, for the most part, taken from the Bible. The Bible nourishes our impetus to prayer and reflection. But there is a deep reservoir of other writings from which we can draw and should do so. However, the stories of the suffering and death of Jesus given to us by Matthew, Mark, Luke and John are seminal and other texts should be used only insofar as they complement what the Gospels present.

The manner of proclaiming the readings must be a

serious concern. Only people who realise that it is the voice and not the page which contains the word of God should be entrusted with proclaiming that word. The readings lend themselves to dramatic presentation and a single voice will be demanded by some texts, whereas a group production will better serve others. Sensitivity to the texts, and to their effective communication, should determine how a reading is offered. The reading of the Passion deserves particularly careful consideration. Planning is of the essence.

PRAYERS

Timing is especially important in the Prayers of Intercession. Clarity and deliberation are the watchwords. We must not be afraid to pause, to allow a few moments for people to make the prayer their own. Often a simple musical response is desirable and effective.

REFLECTIONS

I have included some reflections after some of the readings. These are offered by way of suggestion and should be considered as optional. But some reflection, even a homily, would not be out of place. Again, careful planning will determine what is best for each occasion and each circumstance.

It is my hope that people who use *Walk One Hour* would do so with the greatest freedom to adapt it to what will best serve its purpose. I wish to stimulate study, reflection and prayer around the Cross of Jesus of Nazareth. I am convinced that, in our time and in our place, we need to bring home to ourselves what happened on that dark yet good day so long ago. No one would deny that our world, where we work, where we live, where we play, where we pray, is undergoing a kind of crucifixion. Our time is not a time of hope. Strangely, if we are to discover true hope, we will, I believe, make our discovery at the Place of the Skull, on the hill of Calvary. Our culture, our society, our Churches can be redeemed from the slough of despond into which they have plunged, as so many Gadarene swine, only by the painful paths of study, reflection and prayer. The foot of the Cross is the best place to start.

Jesus is Condemned to Death

BACKGROUND:

Why was Jesus condemned to death? Why crucify someone who, though a thorn in many sides, went about doing good? Sick people were healed, social outcasts and misfits made to feel wanted, sinners converted to new and better ways, stories told of a God who was not a threat but an anxious parent looking for lost souls? Why harm one who did no harm?

There are two answers. There is the Caiaphas/Pilate answer and there is God's answer. That is to say, there is the human answer and there is the divine answer.

The Caiaphas/Pilate answer is furnished by history. It is what happened when two people with different but converging responsibilities had to deal with Jesus of Nazareth and what he stood for. Caiaphas was a priest, the leading priest of the Jewish faith, with responsibility for the running of the Temple in Jerusalem and overseeing the good order of religious Jews everywhere. But, since Rome ruled through its prefect, Pontius Pilate, Caiaphas was responsible to him for the peaceful conduct and good behaviour of Jewish people in Jerusalem and Judaea. Peaceful conduct meant not engaging in revolutionary efforts against Roman authority and good behaviour meant paying swingeing taxes on time. Caiaphas was chief priest for seventeen years and Pilate was prefect for ten of these. They were not pals but each knew where the other stood and they had a viable working relationship.

Jesus claimed to speak of a new kingdom, not the realm of Tiberius Caesar but that of God. What he said and what he did promoted his vision of God and God's authority on earth "as it is in heaven". If God is to take his place on the world's throne, Tiberius must stand down. The challenge to Caiaphas was to keep the fragile peace, and pray under his breath that one day Rome would pass away. The challenge to Pilate was to keep his job. The challenge to Jesus was fearlessly to witness to God's rights in this world. Accordingly, when Jesus instigated a demonstration in the Temple area (the so-called Cleansing of the Temple), Caiaphas and Pilate, quickly and without much of a trial, if any, had him killed. It happened every day of the week, if not in Jerusalem, somewhere else. Routine maintenance.

Then there is God's answer: *God so loved the world that he gave his only son that whosoever believes in him should not perish but have eternal life* (John 3:16). The gospel-makers tried to explain the death of Jesus from the divine perspective, not from the viewpoint of the historian. The historian hopes to tell what happened; the gospel-maker seeks to reveal the finger of God writing in the chaos of human events. So Mark did not set out to tell his readers what happened – they already knew this since they were all Christians. He set out to find the hand of God in the terrible events of the last days of Jesus, by means of giving the God's eye view on the death of Jesus, in order to explain where God was to be found in the many crucifixions inflicted on Rome's Christians by Nero. That is why the trials and condemnation of Jesus are so drawn out in the Gospels, so full of explanation and references to Scripture where God's will might be discerned. Pilate, if he ever met Jesus, wouldn't have wasted two minutes on him. He was that kind of man. It was that kind of world.

But for Mark the man who stood trial was the Son of God. Throughout his story, only God, only Jesus, only supernatural forces (demons), know the secret, the true identity of the man from Nazareth. People cannot fathom the true identity of Jesus until they are willing to stand at the foot of the Cross. In Mark's story no friend of Jesus will be found there. Only a pagan, a Roman centurion, in charge of an execution squad, sees the heart of the matter.

Prayer, reflection, and, with hope, conversion. These are the guides by which Mark leads his readers to Golgotha and to an understanding of what happened there. Such guides turn a routine crucifixion into gospel, good news from God and about God: *Truly, this man was the Son of God.*

DISCUSSION SUGGESTIONS

1. Why was Jesus put to death? Historical (the human point of view) and theological (the God's-eye view) reasons will come to mind. Try to pinpoint which is which as your discussion develops.
2. Would you have given a different verdict if you were (a) Caiaphas, (b) Pilate? Vote as a jury and give your verdict.
3. If the followers of Jesus were on trial today, what would it be for?

Jesus is Condemned to Death

ENTRANCE:

Processional music or appropriate hymn.
Unveiling of the Cross.
Lighting of candles, use of incense, or other appropriate
acts of veneration of the Cross.

OPENING PRAYER RECITED BY ALL:

Almighty God,
be mindful,
we pray you,
of this your family,
for whose sake our Lord Jesus Christ,
when he was betrayed,
did not hesitate to undergo the agony of the Cross.
May our prayerful following in his footsteps
renew in us
our work of faith,
our labour of love,
and our steadfastness of hope.
AMEN.

RESPONSE:

We adore you, O Christ, and we praise you,
because by your holy Cross you have
redeemed the world.

Narrator: They led Jesus to the high priest; and all the chief priests and the elders and scribes were assembled. And Peter followed him at a distance, right into the courtyard of the high priest; and he was sitting with the guards, and warming himself at the fire.

Now the chief priests and the whole council sought testimony against Jesus to put him to death; but they found none. For many bore false witness against him, and their witness did not agree. And some stood up and bore false witness against him, saying,

Voices: We heard him say, "I will destroy this temple that is made with hands, and in three days I will build another, not made with hands."

Narrator: But even on this point their testimony did not agree.

Then the high priest stood up before them and asked Jesus,

High Priest: Have you no answer? What is it that they testify against you?

Narrator: But he was silent and did not answer.

Again the high priest asked him,

High Priest: Are you the Messiah, the Son of the Blessed One?

Narrator: Jesus said:

Jesus: I AM; and you will see the Son of Man seated at the right hand of the Power and coming with the clouds of heaven.

Narrator: Then the high priests tore his garments and said,

High Priest: Why do we need witnesses? You have heard his blasphemy! What is your verdict?

Narrator: All of them condemned him as deserving death. Some began to spit on him, to blindfold him, and to strike him, saying to him, "Prophesy!" The guards also took him over and beat him.

COMMENTARY:

The religious authorities assemble; they will speak for St Mark and, ironically, guide us to the true identity of the prisoner. False evidence there is aplenty. But it is not simply that Jesus spoke against a building, even such a building as the holy Temple. It is not – in God's perspective – for what he said or for what he did that brings Jesus to his death. It is for *who he is*, a new Temple, a new place for God's dwelling. In Jesus beats the heart of God.

SILENT REFLECTION

RESPONSE:

> *Ubi caritas et amor*
> *Ubi caritas, Deus ibi est.*
> *(Where love is, God is.)*

COMMENTARY:

St Mark identifies who is on trial here, who the one in the dock truly is:

Are you the Messiah, the Son of the Blessed One?

Jesus is no mere disturber of the peace, no mere thorn in the side of those who are concerned to uphold Roman imperial authority. The high priest delves deeper. Are you God's authentic voice? Are you, in fact, not only the voice of God but Emmanuel, God-with-us?

The answer shatters all our images of God:

I AM.

God said to Moses, I AM WHO I AM (Exodus 3:14).

Jesus tells that he is of that I AM.

And, further, he is to return to that I AM carrying in his heart God's people from the four corners of the earth (Mark 13:27).

SILENT REFLECTION

HYMN: *Jesus is Lord.*

PRAYERS OF INTERCESSION

LEADER: God so loved us that He gave his Son
to *carry* our sins,
to *bear* the intolerable burdens we place upon ourselves,
to *raise* us out of the terrors we create in our world.

Surely he has borne our griefs and carried our sorrows.
Let us pray, therefore, with confidence that our hearts
may be open to the gospel of the Cross of Jesus.

1. As we follow in the footsteps of Jesus,
let us pray
that our hearts may be opened to the depth and riches
and wisdom of God's love for all peoples.

ALL: Lord, in your mercy, hear our prayer.

2. As we follow in the footsteps of Jesus,
let us pray
that we may persevere in our sufferings,
knowing that suffering produces endurance,
and endurance produces character,
and character produces hope
that does not disappoint,
because God's love has been poured into our hearts.

ALL: Lord, in your mercy, hear our prayer.

3. As we follow in the footsteps of Jesus,
let us pray
that we may confess with our lips
that Jesus Christ is Lord,
and believe in our hearts
that through his death
we are brought to life.

ALL: Lord, in your mercy, hear our prayer.

4. As we follow in the footsteps of Jesus,
let us pray
that we who were estranged from God

but are now reconciled
by the death of his Son,
may be worthy of the gospel of reconciliation
which has been entrusted to us.

ALL: Lord, in your mercy, hear our prayer.

5. Bidding Prayers from the congregation.

ALL: Almighty God,
                          be mindful,
                        we pray you,
                     of this your family,
              for whose sake our Lord Jesus Christ,
                     when he was betrayed,
       did not hesitate to undergo the agony of the Cross.
             May our prayerful following in his footsteps
                          renew in us
                        our work of faith,
                       our labour of love,
                  and our steadfastness of hope.
                            AMEN.

BLESSING:

May the God of steadfastness and encouragement
grant us to live in such harmony with one another,
in accord with Jesus Christ, that together we may
with one voice glorify the God and Father of our
Lord Jesus Christ.

And may the blessing of Almighty God,
Father, Son, and Holy Spirit,
come down upon us,
and remain in our hearts and in our homes forever.

ALL: We adore you, O Christ, and we praise you,
because by your holy Cross you have
redeemed the world.

RECESSIONAL HYMN:

When I survey the wondrous cross…
Isaac Watts (1674–1748)

During the hymn the Cross is covered.
All reverence the Cross and depart.

Jesus Takes Up His Cross

BACKGROUND:

Why do we say Jesus *takes up* his cross?
Why do we not say a cross *is forced upon* Jesus?

Jesus *takes up his cross* is interpretation.
A cross *is forced upon* Jesus is history.

To say that Jesus takes up his cross is to enter into God's understanding of what happened on that dark day. It is to maintain, against all understanding, that Jesus, in obedience to his Father's voice, takes up his cross to accomplish what God wished to reveal through the pain and suffering of that truly blessed day. It is to believe, not what we see before our eyes, but what we hope in our hearts. It is to believe that the burden placed on the shoulders of this young Jew is not only the wood of the cross but the sin of the world. It is to believe that God tells who he is through the cross of his Son. It is to believe that when we see the cross we see into the very heart of God.

To say that a cross is forced on the shoulders of Jesus is to enter into the routine savagery of human oppression. Crucifixion was capital punishment but punishment which carried a fearful message, not only for the victim, but for the casual bystander.

Crucifixion was a public spectacle. Roman citizens, no matter how notoriously criminal, were not put to death by crucifixion (though there were rare exceptions). It was reserved for the under classes and public execution was intended to humiliate the victim, family and friends, and to proclaim, in the most gruesome way imaginable, that Rome ruled.

Rome did not invent crucifixion. With varying degrees of accuracy, ancient sources mention crucifixion among the Assyrians, Celts, Britons and Germans. Herodotus records it as a speciality of the Medes and the Persians and says that Darius crucified 3,000 inhabitants of Babylon. Jews, too, practised crucifixion. The great Jewish historian, Josephus, records that Alexander Jannaeus, who was a Sadducee and the high priest of the Jewish people (103-76 BC), crucified 800 Pharisees and killed their wives and children as the dying men looked on from their crosses.

The Romans increased both the severity and the extent of crucifixion. Their great writer, Cicero, called crucifixion "the most cruel and disgusting penalty". The crucifixion of 6,000 slaves on the Via Appia between Capua and Rome by Crassus, when he eventually managed to defeat Sparticus who led the slave revolt (73-71 BC), is not a figment of Hollywood imagination. And, women, too, were crucified.

Though untold thousands of people were crucified in the ancient world, the remains of only one victim have been found. He was a young Jew, crucified in Jerusalem, sometime in the same century in which Jesus died, and the tale his broken bones have to tell will, in due course, help our understanding of what happened to the young man from Nazareth.

Crucifixion was usually preceded by scourging which, on the one hand, increased the suffering and humiliation of the victim and, on the other, hastened death. Victims were stripped naked, paraded in public, often with a placard around their necks proclaiming their crimes. They were subjected to the sadistic whims of the execution squad which was free to vent its rage and hatred or indulge its sadistic inclinations.

The victim carried a crossbeam, tied to his outstretched arms, impeding progress to the place of execution, especially if that were through narrow streets. Whatever the feelings of onlookers, it was never expedient to show any sympathy for a criminal at the receiving end of Roman justice.

The spectacle of another crucified Jew hardly merited comment, much less remembrance. But the cross of Jesus came to be the Christian sign because the followers of Jesus, deserters every one of them, were transformed by God's power into a new creation. St Paul, who speaks of cross and crucifixion more than any other New Testament writer, explains the difference between history and understanding, between what happened and what really happened, between the wisdom of the world and the foolishness of God, between the power of Caesar and the power of God:

> For the message about the cross
> is foolishness to those who are perishing,
> but to us who are being saved,
> it is the power of God.

For it is written,

"I will destroy the wisdom of the wise,
and the cleverness of the clever, I will defeat."

Isaiah 29:14

Where is the one who is wise?
Where is the scribe?
Where is the debater of this age?
Has not God turned into foolishness
the wisdom of this world?

For since,
in the wisdom of God,
the world did not know God through wisdom,
God decided, through the foolishness of what
    we preach,
to save those who believe.
For Jews demand signs
and Greeks seek wisdom,
but we preach Christ crucified,
a stumbling block to Jews,
and stupidity to Gentiles,
but to those who are called,
both Jews and Greeks,
Christ [is] the power of God
and the wisdom of God.

For God's stupidity is wiser than human wisdom,
and God's weakness is stonger than human strength!

1 Corinthians 1:18-25

St Paul can be difficult to understand but here he is fairly clear. From the human point of view, trying to preach that the death by crucifixion of an insignificant Jew reveals the heart of God is stuff and nonsense. But that is what it is revealed in the death of this man. To the worldly wise, it is mere foolishness. But, to those who have eyes to see, it is the very wisdom of God. And, remember, even when God is "foolish", he is well ahead of our wisdom!

DISCUSSION SUGGESTIONS

1. What messages did imperial Rome convey by the gruesome details of its crucifixion policy?
2. Why did the cross become the Christian sign? Why not an empty coffin?
3. What does the sign of the cross mean (if anything) in your world?

THE SECOND STATION

Jesus Takes Up His Cross

ENTRANCE:

Processional music or appropriate hymn.
Unveiling of the Cross.
Lighting of candles, use of incense, or other appropriate
acts of veneration of the Cross.

OPENING PRAYER RECITED BY ALL:

Almighty God,
be mindful,
we pray you,
of this your family,
for whose sake our Lord Jesus Christ,
when he was betrayed,
did not hesitate to undergo the agony of the Cross.
May our prayerful following in his footsteps
renew in us
our work of faith,
our labour of love,
and our steadfastness of hope.

RESPONSE:

We adore you, O Christ, and we praise you,
because by your holy Cross you have
redeemed the world.

A READING FROM THE PASSION OF ST MARK
Mark 15:1-20

Narrator: As soon as it was morning the chief priests held a consultation with the elders and scribes and the whole council. They bound Jesus, led him away, and handed him over to Pilate. Pilate asked him,

Pilate: Are you the King of the Jews?

Narrator: He answered him,

Jesus: You say so.

Narrator: Then the chief priests accused him of many things. Pilate asked him again,

Pilate: Have you no answer? See how many charges they bring against you.

Narrator: But Jesus made no further reply, so that Pilate was amazed.

Now at the festival Pilate used to release a prisoner for them, anyone for whom they asked. Now a man called Barabbas was in prison with the rebels who had committed murder during the insurrection. So the crowd came and began to ask Pilate to do for them according to his custom. Then he answered them,

Pilate: Do you want me to release for you the King of the Jews?

Narrator: For he realised that it was out of jealousy that the chief priests had handed him over. But the chief priests stirred up the crowd to have him release Barabbas for them instead. Pilate spoke to them again,

Pilate: Then what do you wish me to do with the man you call King of the Jews?

Narrator: They shouted back,

Crowd: Crucify him!

Narrator: Pilate asked them,

Pilate: Why? What evil has he done?

Narrator: But they shouted all the more,

Crowd: Crucify him!

Narrator: So Pilate, wishing to satisfy the crowd, released Barabbas for them; and after flogging Jesus, he handed him over to be crucified.

Then the soldiers led him into the courtyard of the palace (that is, the praetorium); and they called together the whole cohort. And they clothed him in a purple cloak; and after twisting some thorns into a crown, they put it on him. And they began saluting him, "Hail, King of the Jews!" They struck his head with a reed, spat upon him, and knelt down in homage to him. After mocking him, they stripped him of the purple cloak and put his own clothes on him. Then they led him out to crucify him.

COMMENTARY:

The might of Rome condemns Jesus in less time that it takes to read the account of the trial. But St Mark's creative imagination highlights three pointers to God in the rush to get Jesus out of the way.

First, there is the claim that Jesus is King of the Jews. A preposterous claim, as far as Pilate is concerned. A claim deserving crucifixion, according to the chief priests and the crowd they instigate to howl for the prisoner's death.

Secondly, the crowd want the murderer, the terrorist, called Barabbas, set free and the King of the Jews crucified. There is no record and no likelihood that Pilate had a policy of releasing prisoners and certainly not murderers who engaged in insurrection against Roman authority. But Mark's dramatic imagination writes a scene which goes to the very heart of what, from God's point of view, is happening here. Listen:

You alone, you are God, of all the kingdoms of the earth! (2 Kings 19:15)

The Lord has established his throne in the heavens, and his kingdom rules over all. (Psalm 103:19)

Kingship belongs to God! (Obadiah 21)

> How beautiful on the mountains
> are the feet of the messenger
> who announces peace,
> who brings good news [= gospel],
> who announces salvation,
> who says to Zion,
> "Your God reigns!"
>
> Isaiah 52:7

The truth of the matter is that God is King; all others, including King David and King Solomon, are human representatives of God's kingly authority.

To call Jesus "King of the Jews" is, in Mark's view, to go beyond human authority and to claim for Jesus a kingship which is not of this world.

And, thirdly, the murderer in prison is called Barabbas. His name, Bar-Abba, means "Son of the Father". But we recall the voice from heaven, a voice which declared, "This is my beloved Son. Listen to him! (Mark 9:7).

See what words of God are here. The one who is mockingly dressed up as a king, is truly the son of the only true king. The murderer who is called "Son of the Father" is set free, while the true Son of the Father is condemned by Pilate, priests and people.

SILENT REFLECTION

HYMN: *How lovely on the mountains*
                  Leonard E. Smith Jnr

PRAYERS OF INTERCESSION

LEADER:
God so loved us that He gave his Son
to *carry* our sins,
to *bear* the intolerable burdens we place upon ourselves,
to *raise* us out of the terrors we create in our world.

Surely he has borne our griefs
and carried our sorrows.

Let us pray, therefore, with confidence
that our hearts may be open to the gospel of the
Cross of Jesus.

1. As we follow in the footsteps of Jesus,
let us pray
that our hearts may be opened to the depth and riches
and wisdom of God's love for all peoples.

ALL: Lord, in your mercy, hear our prayer.

2. As we follow in the footsteps of Jesus,
let us pray
that we may respect justice,
temper justice with mercy and compassion,
and stand with the innocent unjustly condemned.

ALL: Lord, in your mercy, hear our prayer.

3. As we follow in the footsteps of Jesus,
let us pray
that we may proclaim with our lips
that Jesus Christ is King of our hearts
and that he may reign over
all that we are and all that we do.

ALL: Lord, in your mercy, hear our prayer.

4. As we follow in the footsteps of Jesus,
let us pray
that we who are now reconciled to God
by the death of his Son,
and have been appointed
ministers of reconciliation,

may so conduct ourselves
that we may build the peace of Christ
in our time and in our place.

ALL: Lord, in your mercy, hear our prayer.

5. Bidding Prayers from the congregation.

ALL: Almighty God,
                         be mindful,
                        we pray you,
                     of this your family,
            for whose sake our Lord Jesus Christ,
                    when he was betrayed,
     did not hesitate to undergo the agony of the Cross.
        May our prayerful following in his footsteps
                       renew in us
                     our work of faith,
                    our labour of love,
              and our steadfastness of hope.
                          AMEN

BLESSING:

May the God of steadfastness and encouragement
grant us to live in such harmony with one another,
in accord with Jesus Christ, that together we may
with one voice glorify the God and Father of our
Lord Jesus Christ.

And may the blessing of Almighty God,
Father, Son, and Holy Spirit,
come down upon us,
and remain in our hearts and in our homes forever.

                                          AMEN.

ALL: We adore you, O Christ, and we praise you,
because by your holy Cross you have
redeemed the world.

RECESSIONAL HYMN:

Guide me, O thou great Redeemer
W. Williams (1717-91),
trans. from Welsh P. and W. Williams

During the hymn the Cross is recovered.
All reverence the Cross and depart.

Jesus Falls the First Time

BACKGROUND:

The decree of Pope Clement XII in 1731 fixed the number of stations at fourteen, though one still finds churches with fewer than fourteen and, indeed, in recent times, some parishes have added a fifteenth station to commemorate the resurrection of Jesus. It is, however, instructive to recall that the traditional site(s) of the resurrection in the Basilica of the Holy Sepulchre in Jerusalem is not part of the traditional *Via Dolorosa*.

Nine of the fourteen meditations in the Stations of the Cross are drawn from incidents recorded in one or other of the four Gospels. Five incidents are not found in the Gospels but come from ancient legends and imaginative surmise. They are: the three falls of Jesus, the meeting with his mother and the encounter with Veronica.

It is hardly surprising that Christian imagination should envisage Jesus falling to the ground as he made his painful way to the Place of the Skull. It is easy to see how the tradition of the three falls came to be part of the Way of the Cross. The Franciscans, who had been entrusted with the oversight of the holy places in Jerusalem, had little by way of solid evidence to support their reconstruction of the path of Jesus from the residence of Pilate to Golgotha (remember

that not a stone was left standing on a stone by the
time the Romans had finished flattening the city in
70 AD and again in 135 AD. Emperor Hadrian – the
one who built the eponymous Wall – built a new
city on the graveyard of the old). In order, therefore,
to flesh out the Holy Circulus or Via Dolorosa in
Jerusalem, imagination, not history, determined the
pauses for prayer and reflection as pilgrims made their
way through the streets of the medieval city. If Jesus
had been scourged and beaten up, he would be weakened, and, thus weakened, he would surely have fallen
many times as he was dragged to Golgotha, the place
of execution.

It was usual to scourge criminals before crucifixion
and to subject them, if the execution squad so wished,
to humiliation. That Jesus was subjected to mockery
is mentioned in all four Gospels but the accounts, as
usual, raise historical questions and matters of Christian
interpretation of the events recorded.

There are three mockery scenes in Mark's story
of the passion of Jesus, each involving violence. The
first is at 14:65 when those assembled in the house of
the high priest mock Jesus as a would-be prophet and
the servants inflict blows upon him:

Some began to spit on him, to blindfold him,
and to strike him, saying to him, "Prophesy!"
The guards also took him over and beat him.

Mark 14:65

The words used to describe this incident fulfil to the letter the details the prophet Jesus had foretold about his final ordeal:

> … they will mock him, and spit upon him, and flog him, and kill him, and after three days he will rise again.   Mark 10:34

There is the added irony that, as Jesus is being mocked, derided and beaten, the prophetical words spoken by Jesus concerning Peter's denial are, at that very moment, coming to pass in the courtyard of the high priest's residence ("Amen I say to you, this day, this very night, before the cock crows twice, you will deny me three times" – Mark 14:30). Thus the rough treatment meted out to Jesus serves to confirm his status as prophet and the truthfulness of his claim to belong to God's I AM.

The same may be said of the second mockery in the courtyard of Pilate's residence in the palace of Herod the Great. The scene is so constructed that the inflicted insult and injury not only draw the reader into sympathetic solidarity with the victim but also reveal the true identity of the one so sorely abused. The cohort of soldiers – that's 600 men – dress Jesus in a mockery of imperial robes and insignia and greet him, "Hail, King of the Jews!" It is, of course, a parody of the imperial greeting, "Hail, Caesar!" And the taunting culminates with an act of mock worship.

The scene contains echoes – distant but discernible – of two passages from a section of the Book of Isaiah often called the Songs of the Suffering Servant. These poems are not prophecies concerning Jesus but early Christians saw them as appropriate to describe the sufferings of Jesus:

> He was despised and rejected by men;
> a man of suffering
> and acquainted with infirmity;
> and, as one from whom men hide their faces,
> he was despised, and we esteemed him not.
> Surely he has borne our griefs
> and carried our sorrow;
> yet we accounted him stricken,
> smitten by God and afflicted.
> But he was wounded for our transgressions,
> he was crushed for our iniquities;
> upon him was the punishment that made us whole.
> By his bruises we are healed.
>
> Isaiah 53:3-5

Early Christians meditated on such passages from the ancient Scriptures and saw in God's words a fitting description of the fate of God's Son. But we must be open to the possibility that the quotations from the Old Testament have so influenced the telling of incidents in such detail that we can have no certainty that we can recover exactly what really happened. Interpretation has so embroidered the facts of history that the facts have all but vanished from view.

Yet we can detect the ironies in these mockeries and beatings. A common criminal is routinely beaten up and made the butt of cruel humiliation. But the very mockery itself reveals that the victim is truly a prophet, truly, the King of Israel, truly the Son of God. All this is revealed in God's holy words which lead us to the real truth of what we see before our eyes.

The third mockery takes place as Jesus dies upon his cross. It, too, as we shall see, is a revelation of who God is, the God that so loved the world that he offered us his own Son to do with as only we humans know how.

The betrayal by Judas Iscariot, the first of the chosen Twelve to fall, is more shocking than the mockery of enemies. For Judas betrays trust and friendship in the fellowship of a meal and with the intimacy of a kiss:

> And when it was evening [Jesus] came with the twelve. And as they were at table eating, Jesus said, "Truly, I say to you, one of you will betray me, one who is eating with me."
>
> Mark 14:17-18

And:

> Now the betrayer had given them a sign, saying, "The one I shall kiss is the man; seize him and lead him away." And when he came, he went up to him at once, and said, "Master!" And he kissed him.
>
> Mark 14:44-45

The first and deepest fall.

DISCUSSION SUGGESTIONS

1. How does the routine humiliation of Jesus by bored soldiers offer amazing insights into the true identity of the victim? Can you spot the irony of the situation?
2. Why, do you think, Judas Iscariot, one of the Twelve, betrayed Jesus?
3. Mockery often follows pretension. For what pretensions are Christians (rightly or wrongly) mocked in your world?

Jesus Falls the First Time

ENTRANCE:

Processional music or appropriate hymn.
Unveiling of the Cross.
Lighting of candles, use of incense, or other appropriate
acts of veneration of the Cross.

OPENING PRAYER RECITED BY ALL:

Almighty God,
be mindful,
we pray you,
of this your family,
for whose sake our Lord Jesus Christ,
when he was betrayed,
did not hesitate to undergo the agony of the Cross.
May our prayerful following in his footsteps
renew in us
our work of faith,
our labour of love,
and our steadfastness of hope.

RESPONSE:

We adore you, O Christ, and we praise you,
because by your holy Cross you have
redeemed the world.

[Judas at the Supper]

Narrator: When it was evening, Jesus came with the Twelve. And as they were at the table eating, Jesus said,

Jesus: Truly I tell you, one of you will betray me, one who is eating with me.

Narrator: They began to be sorrowful, and to say to him one after another,

The Twelve: Is it I?

Narrator: He said to them,

Jesus: It is one of the Twelve, one who is dipping bread in the same dish with me. For the Son of Man goes as it is written of him, but woe to that man by whom the Son of man is betrayed! It would have been better for that man if he had not been born.

COMMENTARY:

Jesus falls on his way to Calvary. His falls are the heavier because of other falls along the way. Not least, the fall of Judas, one of the Twelve.

The Twelve, hand-picked by Jesus to be with him and to be sent out bearing Jesus and his gospel in their hearts (Mark 3:13-19). They embodied in a public way and as a permanent lesson what Jesus meant by discipleship. And at the heart of this intimacy and trust was Judas, the one who betrayed him.

SILENT REFLECTION

A READING FROM THE PASSION OF ST MARK
Mark 14:43-46
[Judas at the Arrest of Jesus]

Narrator: And immediately, while he was still speaking, Judas came, one of the Twelve, and with him a crowd with swords and clubs, from the chief priests and the scribes and elders. Now the betrayer had given them a sign, saying,

Judas: The one I shall kiss is the man; seize him and lead him away securely.

Narrator: And when he came, he went up to him at once, and said,

Judas: Master!

Narrator: And he kissed him. And they laid their hands on him and seized him.

COMMENTARY:

The intimacy of sharing a meal, the love and affection of a kiss, here are the signs of betrayal. They had promised to give him money (Mark 14:10-11) and, for that, he handed Jesus into their hands. Only Judas can tell why and what brought him to such a fall from decency, friendship, responsibility, and, indeed, love.

PRAYERS OF INTERCESSION

LEADER:
God so loved us that He gave his Son
to *carry* our sins,
to *bear* the intolerable burdens we place upon ourselves,
to *raise* us out of the terrors we create in our world.
Surely he has borne our griefs
and carried our sorrows.
Let us pray, therefore, with confidence
that our hearts may be open to the gospel of the
Cross of Jesus.

1. As we follow in the footsteps of Jesus,
let us pray
that our hearts may be opened to the depth and riches
and wisdom of God's love for all peoples.

ALL: Lord, in your mercy, hear our prayer.

2. As we follow in the footsteps of Jesus,
let us pray
that we may persevere in our sufferings,
knowing that suffering produces endurance,
and endurance produces character,
and character produces hope
that does not disappoint,
because God's love has been poured into our hearts.

ALL: Lord, in your mercy, hear our prayer.

3. As we follow in the footsteps of Jesus,
let us pray
that our faith may not be compromised
by betrayal,
by self-seeking,
by the pursuit of wealth,
or fleeting pleasure.

ALL: Lord, in your mercy, hear our prayer.

4. As we follow in the footsteps of Jesus,
let us pray
that our hearts may be open
to God's forgiveness,
that we may not be crushed
by the burdens of our weaknesses.

ALL: Lord, in your mercy, hear our prayer.

5. Bidding Prayers from the congregation.

ALL: Almighty God,
                be mindful,
                we pray you,
                of this your family,
        for whose sake our Lord Jesus Christ,
                when he was betrayed,
    did not hesitate to undergo the agony of the Cross.
        May our prayerful following in his footsteps
                renew in us
                our work of faith,
                our labour of love,
            and our steadfastness of hope.
                    AMEN.

BLESSING:

May the God of steadfastness and encouragement
grant us to live in such harmony with one another,
in accord with Jesus Christ, that together we may
with one voice glorify the God and Father of our
Lord Jesus Christ.

And may the blessing of Almighty God,
Father, Son, and Holy Spirit,
come down upon us,
and remain in our hearts and in our homes forever.

AMEN.

ALL: We adore you, O Christ, and we praise you,
because by your holy Cross you have
redeemed the world.

RECESSIONAL HYMN:

God of Mercy and Compassion
E. Vaughan (1827-1908)

During the Hymn the Cross is covered.
All venerate the Cross and depart.

Jesus Meets His Heartbroken Mother

BACKGROUND:

St John's Gospel tells of the Mother of Jesus (whom he does not name) at the foot of the Cross. None of the four Gospels record a meeting of Jesus and his mother on the way to Golgotha.

Mary is mentioned in St Mark's Gospel in two passages which raise many questions and challenge our unquestioning and, perhaps, sentimental view of Jesus and his family. In Mark 3:31–35 we learn that "the mother of Jesus and his brothers" came to where Jesus was addressing a large crowd, and, standing at the edge of the crowd, they passed a message and Jesus was told, "Your mother and your brothers [and your sisters] are outside, asking for you." In a second passage, Mark 6:3, Mary is named and so are family members: "Is not this the carpenter, the son of Mary and the brother of James and Joses and Judas and Simon, and are not his sisters here with us?" The precise relationship of these brothers and sisters to Jesus remains a matter of controversy. But the reply of Jesus to the message from his family defines the true basis of closeness to Jesus:

> And looking around on those who sat about him, he said, "Here are my mother and my brothers! Whoever does the will of God is my brother, and sister, and mother.　　Mark 3:34-35

Therein lies the greatness of Mary. She is, pre-eminently, the one who hears the word of God, ponders it in her heart, and does it. It is, therefore, entirely appropriate that Christian tradition should picture the Mother of Jesus meeting with her Son on his journey to an ignominious death. That is the hardest word of all to hear and to ponder in the heart. The scene of Mary meeting her son carrying his cross of shame and defeat may have sprung from Christian imagination with little by way of historical foundation. But Christian imagination has here come to the heart of the matter and to the heart of Mary whose discipleship does not waver. Jesus on any road other than the road which leads to the Place of the Skull is unrecognisable. A Christian vision which revels in the empty tomb and the Risen Jesus, all the while ignoring the way of the Cross and the agony of death has lost sight of where God is to be found in the story. As ever, Mary, unerringly, points to where her son is to be found.

Crucifixion was an instrument of terror. As such, there was little sympathy expressed for its victims. Whatever the personal feelings of family and friends, they were punished by public humiliation and terrorised into silence. To help the criminal was to condone the crime. Every facet of the process of crucifixion was intended to drive a wedge between the victim and his family and friends and to damn the cause for which he was sentenced. It is easy to kill criminals. It is the way in which they are killed which turns their death into an act of terror, a public and unmistakeable warning to the living of where power lies and how terrible the consequences for those who would gainsay it.

None of the Stations of the Cross have a word to say about Peter, Andrew, James and John or any of the men who followed Jesus and became part of the intimate band, known as the Twelve, on whose shoulders Jesus placed such responsibility and in whose courage he invested so much hope. It is the women in the Gospels who are to be found in at the death and it is the women who are first at the empty tomb and who first are greeted by the Risen Lord. Historically speaking, we are on sure ground here. It must have been difficult, in that man's world, to remember and then to record of the men who travelled to Jerusalem that "they all forsook him, and fled" (Mark 14:50). Mark names the women who journeyed with Jesus and who did not run away:

> There were also women looking from afar,
> among whom were Mary Magdalene, and Mary
> the mother of James the younger and of Joses,
> and Salome, who, when he was in Galilee,
> followed him, and ministered to him; and also
> many other women who came up with him to
> Jerusalem.
>
> Mark 15:40-41

These women may have stood afar off. But they were there and we will do well to pay attention to their presence for they will point us unerringly to God.

DISCUSSION SUGGESTIONS

1. Only in St John's Gospel do we find the mother of Jesus at the foot of the Cross. We also find her at a wedding in Cana (John 2:1–12). Can you detect similarities between the two scenes?
2. Why is St Mark's account of Jesus dying on the cross devoid of friends or even of a single compassionate word (unlike St Luke)?
3. Why do some Christians (Catholic and Orthodox, for examples) honour Mary more than others?

THE FOURTH STATION

Jesus Meets His Heartbroken Mother

ENTRANCE:

HYMN: *Stabat Mater* (verses 1–5)
                     Jacopone da Todi (d.1306)

Unveiling of the Cross.
Lighting of candles, use of incense, or other appropriate
acts of veneration of the Cross.

OPENING PRAYER RECITED BY ALL:

Almighty God,
be mindful,
we pray you,
of this your family,
for whose sake our Lord Jesus Christ,
when he was betrayed,
did not hesitate to undergo the agony of the Cross.
May our prayerful following in his footsteps
renew in us
our work of faith,
our labour of love,
and our steadfastness of hope.

RESPONSE:

We adore you, O Christ, and we praise you,
because by your holy Cross you have
redeemed the world.

A READING FROM THE GOSPEL OF ST MARK
Mark 3:31-35

Narrator: And the mother of Jesus and his brothers came; and standing outside they sent to him and called him. And a crowd was sitting about him; and they said to him,

Crowd: Your mother and your brothers [and your sisters] are outside asking for you.

Narrator: And he replied,

Jesus: Who are my mother and my brothers [and my sisters]?

Narrator: And looking around on those who sat about him, he said,

Jesus: Here are my mother and brothers! Whoever does the will of God is my brother, and sister, and mother.

COMMENTARY:

Doing the will of God has brought Mother and Son to the terror of crucifixion. The peasants from Nazareth, caught in the web of intrigue and power, have come to this: another crucifixion, another shattered family, another grieving mother. Yet this routine brutality, for both mother and son, is a way into the very mystery of God. Jesus had said "to those who were about him with the Twelve" to those, that is, who had ears to hear, that to them, and not to those outside, would be given "the secret of the kingdom of God" (Mark 4:10-11). And the secret, the mystery, of God's will being done, of God's kingdom coming to earth is this:

Behold,
we are going up to Jerusalem;
and the Son of man
will be delivered to the chief priests and the
scribes,
and they will condemn him to death,
and deliver him to the Gentiles;
and they will mock him
and spit upon him,
and scourge him,
and kill him;
and after three days he will rise.

Mark 10:33-34

It is in this meeting that the mother will come truly to know her son and her son truly to know his mother.

SILENT REFLECTION

HYMN: *Stabat Mater*
(verses 14-16)

LEADER: God so loved us that He gave his Son
to *carry* our sins,
to *bear* the intolerable burdens we place upon ourselves,
to *raise* us out of the terrors we create in our world.
Surely he has borne our griefs
and carried our sorrows.

Let us pray, therefore, with confidence that our hearts
may be open to the gospel of the Cross of Jesus.

1. As we follow in the footsteps of Jesus and Mary,
let us pray
that our hearts may be opened to the depth and riches
and wisdom of God's love for all peoples.

ALL: Lord, in your mercy, hear our prayer.

2. As we follow in the footsteps of Jesus and Mary,
let us pray
that we may keep true to God's commandments,
and bear witness to the secret of God's kingdom
which has been made known to us
by the death and resurrection of His Son.

ALL: Lord, in your mercy, hear our prayer.

3. As we follow in the footsteps of Jesus and Mary,
let us pray
that evil may be overcome,
and that the earth may rejoice in God's love
poured out for us in the Blood of the Lamb.

ALL: Lord, in your mercy, hear our prayer.

4. As we follow in the footsteps of Jesus and Mary,
let us pray
that we who are now reconciled to God
by the death of his Son,
and have been appointed
ministers of reconciliation,
may so conduct ourselves
that we may build the peace of Christ
in our time and in our place.

ALL: Lord, in your mercy, hear our prayer.

5. Bidding Prayers from the congregation.

ALL: Almighty God,
                   be mindful,
                  we pray you,
               of this your family,
        for whose sake our Lord Jesus Christ,
             when he was betrayed,
    did not hesitate to undergo the agony of the Cross.
        May our prayerful following in his footsteps
                  renew in us
                our work of faith,
               our labour of love,
            and our steadfastness of hope.
                   AMEN.

BLESSING:

May the God of steadfastness and encouragement
grant us to live in such harmony with one another,
in accord with Jesus Christ, that together we may
with one voice glorify the God and Father of our
Lord Jesus Christ.

And may the blessing of Almighty God,
Father, Son, and Holy Spirit,
come down upon us,
and remain in our hearts and in our homes forever.

AMEN.

ALL: We adore you, O Christ, and we praise you,
         because by your holy Cross you have
                  redeemed the world.

RECESSIONAL HYMN:

Stabat Mater (verses 17-20)

During the hymn the Cross is covered.
All reverence the Cross and depart.

Simon of Cyrene Helps Jesus to Carry His Cross

BACKGROUND:

The image of Simon of Cyrene carrying the cross of Jesus is a comforting one. We may not wish to intrude into the poignant meeting of Mother and Son but we can see ourselves in Simon, in Veronica and in the women of Jerusalem. It is, however, dangerous to allow piety and wishful thinking to run ahead of realities. It is all too easy to sanitise the death of Jesus of Nazareth.

The four Gospels report that Jesus carried his cross (*stauros*). Contemporaries would have understood this to mean that Jesus went to death carrying only the crossbeam (the *partibulum* or *antenna*). It was carried behind the nape of the neck, with the arms pulled back, hooked over it and tied in place. The *stipes* or *staticulum*, the vertical part of the cross, was implanted at the place of execution (indeed, in might be an old tree). There would, therefore, be no reason to press-gang someone into carrying a beam already strapped to the victim's shoulders. St John's Gospel – pointedly – says "they took Jesus, and he went out, *bearing his own cross*" (John 19:17). There is plenty of evidence that it would not have been normal Roman practice to force someone or to allow a volunteer to carry the crossbeam of a criminal. And Mark records that the soldiers forced Simon to carry the cross beam. He was not a volunteer.

Was Simon a Jew? His name is Greek, though it served as the Greek form of the Jewish name Simeon. He was from Cyrene, the capital city of the district of Cyrenica in Libya (North Africa). There was a colony of Jews there and they had a synagogue. That this community kept in close contact with Jerusalem is clear from the fact that there was a Cyrenian synagogue in Jerusalem (Acts of the Apostles 6:9). Did Simon of Cyrene belong to this community, having settled on some land near Jerusalem? Mark tells that he was "coming in from the country" (Mark 15:21).

His sons bear a Greek name (Alexander) and a Latin name (Rufus). They seem to have been known to the first readers of Mark's Gospel. Otherwise, it seems pointless to mention them. An early first-century AD ossuary was discovered in a burial cave on the south-western slope of the Kidron Valley outside Jerusalem in 1941. It appears that the cave was used as a burial place by a Jewish family from Cyrene. An inscription on the ossuary reads "Alexander, son of Simon". Is this no more than a coincidence?

There are New Testament references to a Rufus (Romans 16:13), to an Alexander (1 Timothy 1:20; 2 Timothy 4:14), to Cyrene and Cyrenians (Acts of the Apostles 2:10; 6:9; 11:20; 13:1). Christian imagination glamorised the sons of Simon and made them bishops. Give early Christians an inch and they usually went the extra mile. However, there is nothing inherently impossible in the supposition that there was a Jewish family from Cyrene which settled in Jerusalem and converted to Christianity.

History and interpretation. The history is difficult to tie down but there may be good reason to be confident of why Mark records that Simon was compelled to carry the cross of Jesus. Much of Mark's Gospel is concerned with the failure of the Twelve and other disciples to understand Jesus and to align themselves unreservedly to his destiny. Uncompromisingly, Jesus spells out what is required of all would-be followers:

> And he called to him the crowd with his
> disciples, and said to them, "If any man would
> come after me, let him deny himself and take
> up his cross and follow me."
>
> Mark 8:34

Given the horror of crucifixion and its attendant humiliations, this is an appalling invitation. It may well be that the centurion and his soldiers feared that Jesus was so weak that he would not make it to the Place of the Skull outside the walls of the city, and that they compelled the unfortunate Simon to carry the cross beam in order to ensure that their orders from Pilate were carried out to the letter. And it may be, too, that the wood of the Cross spoke as eloquently to Simon as it did to an Anglo-Saxon follower of Jesus who lived nearer to our time and our place and whose meditation on the Cross, *The Dream of the Rood*, may still move our hearts.

DISCUSSION SUGGESTIONS

1. The Gospels of Matthew, Mark, and Luke, insist that the soldiers compelled Simon of Cyrene to carry the cross. Why do you think Christians tend to picture Simon as willingly stepping forward to help Jesus?
2. Why does St John's Gospel omit the story of Simon?
3. Jesus is reported to have told his followers that they must take up their cross everyday and follow him. Does this command have any meaning today?

Simon of Cyrene Helps Jesus to Carry His Cross

ENTRANCE:

Processional music or appropriate hymn.
Unveiling of the Cross.
Lighting of candles, use of incense, or other appropriate
acts of veneration of the Cross.

OPENING PRAYER RECITED BY ALL:

Almighty God,
be mindful,
we pray you,
of this your family,
for whose sake our Lord Jesus Christ,
when he was betrayed,
did not hesitate to undergo the agony of the Cross.
May our prayerful following in his footsteps
renew in us
our work of faith,
our labour of love,
and our steadfastness of hope.

RESPONSE:

We adore you, O Christ, and we praise you,
because by your holy Cross you have
redeemed the world.

Narrator: Jesus began to teach them that the Son of man must suffer many things, and be rejected by the elders and the chief priests and the scribes, and be killed, and after three days rise again. And he said this plainly. And Peter took him, and began to rebuke him. But turning and seeing his disciples, he rebuked Peter, and said,

Jesus: Get behind me, Satan! For you are not on the side of God but of men.

Narrator: And he called to him the crowd with his disciples, and said to them,

Jesus: If any man would follow after me, let him deny himself and take up his cross and follow me. For whoever would save his life will lose it; and whoever loses his life for my sake and the gospel's will save it. For what does it profit a man to gain the whole world and forfeit his life? For what can a man give in return for his life? For whoever is ashamed of me and of my words in this adulterous and sinful generation, of him will the Son of man also be ashamed, when he comes in the glory of the Father with his holy angels.

A READING FROM THE GOSPEL OF ST MARK
Mark15:21

Narrator: And they compelled a passer-by, Simon of Cyrene, who was coming in from the country, the father of Alexander and Rufus, to carry his cross.

COMMENTARY:

Doing the will of God has brought Mother and Son to the terror of crucifixion. Merely passing by has brought Simon of Cyrene to the terror of crucifixion. Doing the will of God brings all would-be followers to the terror of crucifixion. Life compels crucifixion. A sword pierces all human hearts, at least, all hearts that are not hardened to compassion, deaf to suffering, and blind to pain. Simon, minding his own business, was compelled to carry the cross. So are we all.

SILENT REFLECTION

HYMN: *When I survey the wondrous Cross...*
                    Isaac Watts (1674–1748)

AN OLD ENGLISH POEM
The Dream of the Rood

I will tell a marvellous vision
dreamed at the dead of night,
when speech-gifted men were sleeping.
I thought I saw the wondrous tree
moving in high and wrapped in light,
the most shining cross.
All that glowing sign was streaming with gold
gems were set
beautiful at its foot,
five were on the cross-beam ...

Glorious was the cross of victory,
and I stained with sin
and wounded with iniquities ...
They stripped the young Hero that was God Almighty,
He mounted the high cross,
courageous,
a vision to many,
that he might redeem all folk.
I trembled as that Man embraced me;
yet I dared not bend earthwards
nor fall to the ground;
I had to stand firm.

I the Cross was raised;
aloft I held the powerful King,
the Lord of Heaven;
I dared not bow down.
They pierced me with dark nails;
on me can be seen the scars,
open malicious wounds;
I dared not harm one of them.
They mocked us both together.
I was all flowing with blood
pouring from the Man's side,
when he had sent his spirit on before.

SILENT REFLECTION

HYMN: *Keep in mind that Jesus Christ has died for us...*
                              Lucien Deiss

LEADER: God so loved us that He gave his Son
to *carry* our sins,
to *bear* the intolerable burdens we place upon ourselves,
to *raise* us out of the terrors we create in our world.
Surely he has borne our griefs and carried our sorrows.
Let us pray, therefore, with confidence that our hearts
may be open to the gospel of the Cross of Jesus.

1. As we follow in the footsteps of Jesus,
let us pray
that our hearts may be opened to the depth and riches
and wisdom of God's love for all peoples.

ALL: Lord, in your mercy, hear our prayer.

2. As we follow in the footsteps of Jesus,
let us pray
that we may take up our cross
and witness to the gospel
in the pursuit of justice and peace in our world.

ALL: Lord, in your mercy, hear our prayer.

3. As we follow in the footsteps of Jesus,
let us pray
for all who carry the cross
of famine,
of war,
and disease.

ALL: Lord, in your mercy, hear our prayer.

4. As we follow in the footsteps of Jesus,
let us pray
that we who are now reconciled to God
by the death of his Son,
and have been appointed
ministers of reconciliation,
may so conduct ourselves
that we may build the peace of Christ
in our time and in our place.

ALL: Lord, in your mercy, hear our prayer.

5. Bidding Prayers from the congregation.

ALL: Almighty God,
                    be mindful,
                  we pray you,
              of this your family,
        for whose sake our Lord Jesus Christ,
              when he was betrayed,
    did not hesitate to undergo the agony of the Cross.
       May our prayerful following in his footsteps
                  renew in us
               our work of faith,
               our labour of love,
          and our steadfastness of hope.
                    AMEN.

BLESSING:

May the God of steadfastness and encouragement grant
that we may live in such harmony with one another,
in accord with Jesus Christ, that together we may
with one voice glorify the God and Father of our
Lord Jesus Christ.

And may the blessing of Almighty God,
Father, Son, and Holy Spirit,
come down upon us,
and remain in our hearts and in our homes forever.

AMEN.

ALL: We adore you, O Christ, and we praise you,
          because by your holy Cross you have
          redeemed the world.

RECESSIONAL HYMN:

Breathe on me, Breath of God
Edwin Hatch (1835-89)

During the hymn the Cross is covered.
All reverence the Cross and depart.

Veronica Wipes the Face of Jesus

BACKGROUND:

The story of Veronica has little to do with history and everything to do with prayer, reflection and discipleship. It well illustrates the Christian determination to seek the meaning of what really happened on the *Via Dolorosa*, the Road of Sorrow. There was little need for the followers of Jesus to imagine what crucifixion and its terrors involved; it was a part of everyday experience, an instrument of state terror, effective because it was visible. The Cross became the Christian sign because Christian faith saw there a God who suffered with the pain of the world, a God not only dying for the people of the world but with the people of the world. On the way to Golgotha Christians saw God going before and wayleaving a path of hope and peace and safety. The instinct to be part of the drama, to ask *Were you there when they crucified my Lord?*, the impulse of compassion, flowered in the story of Veronica.

The story probably begins with the account given by St Luke of some women mourning for Jesus as he passes by (Luke 23:27-31). These are the women of the Eighth Station. In time imagination singled out one of them and she became, in Christian storytelling, Berenice or, to give her name in Latin, Veronica.

There is an old Greek document called The Acts

of Pilate. It survives in many medieval manuscripts and in many languages, notably in Latin, Coptic, Syriac, Armenian and Arabic, proof of its popularity. It probably was written in the second century AD. The work gives an account of the trial of Jesus before Pilate, depending heavily on the Gospels of Matthew and John. This lengthy account not only sets out to establish the innocence of Jesus but also the innocence of Pilate. Many of the people Jesus cured are brought before the governor and testify to the goodness and greatness of Jesus, among them the invalid who had been afflicted for thirty-eight years (John 5:1-9) and a blind man (Mark 10:46-52). Then a woman gives evidence:

> And a woman called Bernice [Latin: Veronica] crying out from a distance said: "I had an issue of blood and I touched the hem of his garment, and the issue of blood, which had lasted twelve years, ceased."

> The Acts of Pilate VII

This woman is, of course, the woman with severe haemorrhaging who is healed when she touches Jesus' clothes (Mark 5:24-34). The Church historian, Eusebius (265-340 AD), bishop of Caesarea-by-the-Sea, reports that there was a bronze statue outside Bernice's house in Caesarea Philippi, depicting a kneeling woman before the figure of Jesus, whose hands were extended in a healing gesture.

In another document, *Mors Pilati* [The Death of

Pilate], Emperor Tiberius is imagined to be ill and he sends an emissary to Pilate to have the miracle-working Jesus heal him. But Jesus is already dead and the best that can be done is to send to Rome a woman named Veronica who had met Jesus and who possesses a linen cloth on which was imprinted the face of the Saviour. Veronica's meeting with Jesus, in this account, does not take place on the way to Calvary. And, incidentally, Tiberius is healed.

All of this is fiction and all of it lies behind the poignant scene of the woman Veronica meeting with Jesus and wiping his face as he goes to death. Pious legend is not, however, to be dismissed as of no account. It witnesses to the Christian instinct to participate in the sufferings and death of Jesus, imaginatively to reflect, to pray, and to learn discipleship. Veronica, whose name means *the bearer of true icon*, stands with all who seek to be Christ-bearers in our time and in our place.

DISCUSSION SUGGESTIONS

1. Should we be uneasy that early Christians present us with fictional characters and stories even in the very prayers and meditations we make at the foot of the cross?
2. Great artists meditate on the death of Jesus and fill our minds and hearts with enduring images.

Consider *The Crucifixion* by Mathias Grunewald, *The Crowning with Thorns*, by Hieronymus Bosch, *The Scourging* by Diego Velazquez. If there are Stations of the Cross in your church, discuss their artistic merit (if any).

3. How do Christians in our time and place present the suffering and death of Jesus? Should we emphasise the resurrection of Jesus more than his suffering and death?

Veronica Wipes the Face of Jesus

ENTRANCE:

Processional Music or appropriate hymn.
Unveiling of the Cross.
Lighting of candles, use of incense, or other appropriate
acts of veneration of the Cross.

OPENING PRAYER RECITED BY ALL:

Almighty God,
be mindful,
we pray you,
of this your family,
for whose sake our Lord Jesus Christ,
when he was betrayed,
did not hesitate to undergo the agony of the Cross.
May our prayerful following in his footsteps
renew in us
our work of faith,
our labour of love,
and our steadfastness of hope.

RESPONSE:

We adore you, O Christ, and we praise you,
because by your holy Cross you have
redeemed the world.

A READING FROM ST PAUL'S LETTER
TO THE PHILIPPIANS
Philippians 2:1-11

READER:
So if there is any encouragement in Christ,
any incentive of love,
any participation in the Spirit,
and affection and sympathy,
complete my joy by being of the same mind,
having the same love,
being in full accord and of one mind.
Do nothing from selfishness nor conceit,
but in humility count others better than yourselves.
Let each one of you look not only to his own
interests,
but also to the interests of others.

Have this mind among yourselves,
which you have in Christ Jesus,
who, though he was in the form of God,
did not count equality with God
a thing to be exploited for personal gain,
but emptied himself,
taking the form of a slave,
being born in the human likeness.
And being found in human likeness,
he humbled himself
and became obedient unto death,
even death on a cross.

Therefore God has highly exalted him
and bestowed on him the name which is
above every name,
that at the name of Jesus
every knee should bow,
in heaven and on earth and under the earth,
and every tongue confess
that Jesus Christ is Lord,
to the glory of God the Father.

COMMENTARY:

The first humiliation of God's Son is the humiliation of entering into the world of our humanity, of becoming a slave to all that mortal flesh is heir to: to weakness, to fallibility, to frailty. A second humiliation follows on the first. Not only did the Son become the slave but he gave his life into the hands of sinful men who crucified him. But through that emptying of himself, Christ has resumed his God-likeness and been named by God as Lord of all. Let every tongue confess that Jesus Christ is Lord!

REFLECTION AND PRAYER:

1. We know that in everything God works for good
with those who love him,
who are called according to his purpose.
For those whom he forenew
he also predestined
to be conformed to the *image* of his Son.
Romans 8:28-29

RESPONSE: [sung]   *Jesus is Lord*

2. And we all,
with unveiled face,
beholding the glory of the Lord,
are being changed into his *image*,
from one degree of glory to another;
for this comes from the Lord who is Spirit .

2 Corinthians 3:18

RESPONSE: *Jesus is Lord*

3. Therefore put to death what is earthly in you:
immorality
impurity,
passion,
evil desire ,
and covetousness,
which is idolatry.
On account of these the wrath of God is coming.
In these you once walked, when you lived in them.
But now put them all away:
anger,
wrath,
malice,
slander,
and foul talk from your mouth.
Do not lie to one another,
seeing that you have put off the old nature with its
practices
and have put on the new nature,
which is being renewed in knowledge

after the *image* of its creator,
Christ who is Lord of all.
Colossians 3:5-11

RESPONSE: *Jesus is Lord*

ALL: Almighty God,
                 be mindful,
                 we pray you,
                 of this your family,
        for whose sake our Lord Jesus Christ,
                 when he was betrayed,
did not hesitate to undergo the agony of the Cross.
        May our prayerful following in his footsteps
                 renew in us
                 our work of faith,
             and our steadfastness of hope.
                 AMEN.

BLESSING:

May the God of steadfastness and encouragement
grant that we may live in such harmony with one
another, in accord with Jesus Christ, that together
we may with one voice glorify the God and Father
of our Lord Jesus Christ.

And may the blessing of Almighty God,
Father, Son, and Holy Spirit,
come down upon us,
and remain in our hearts and in our homes forever.
                              AMEN.

ALL: We adore you, O Christ, and we praise you,
        because by your holy Cross you have
            redeemed the world.

RECESSIONAL HYMN:

> *O Sacred Head sore wounded*
> Paulus Gerhardt (1607–76)

During the hymn the Cross is covered.
All reverence the Cross and depart.

Jesus Falls the Second Time

BACKGROUND:

The three falls of Jesus are not told in the Gospels but the brutality of crucifixion does not require imagination to add to its horrors. Christian prayer and reflection have always seen in the falls of Jesus a counterpoint to human failure, to falls from grace, to infidelities, weak resolve and betrayal. St Mark, too, was well aware that the faithful, steadfast determination of Jesus to face death was in stark contrast to those who forsook him and fled (Mark 14:50). Chief among the fallen was Peter.

Mark may well have been a companion of Simon Peter. Yet his portrait of the fisherman is painted almost unremittingly in dark and sombre colours. The "trial" of Peter by the servant girl and those standing around takes almost as long to tell as the trial of Jesus before Pilate. But while Jesus resolutely proclaims I AM, Peter is equally emphatic: I AM NOT.

In the beginning, Simon and Andrew (and nobody else in the Gospels) were called to become "fishers of men" (Mark 1:16-17), and they are named first in the call of the Twelve, that symbolic re-creation of the Twelve Tribes of Israel and an earnest of the nation's destiny (Mark 3:13-19). We watch with Simon Peter and the rest as Jesus preaches and heals and enter their learning curve, a curve which is tested at Caesarea Philippi:

And Jesus went on with his disciples, to the
villages of Caesarea Philippi; and on the way
he asked his disciples, "Who do people say
that I am?" And they told him, "John the
Baptist; and others say, Elijah; and others one
of the prophets." And he asked them, "But
who do you say that I am?" Peter answered
him: "You are the Messiah." And he charged
them to tell no one about him.

Mark 8:27-30

But as soon as Jesus pointed out that being the Messiah,
being the Christ, meant enduring death on a cross,
Peter refused to accept God's ordering of the fate of
Jesus, and, from that moment, the commitment of
the fisherman to Jesus deteriorated and ended in
cursing, swearing, and denial. The story of Peter in St
Mark's Gospel is the story of a fall and Mark gives
little sign of recovery.

Yet we know that Peter did recover. We know a
little (but very little) of his place in the first group of
Christians to form after the resurrection of Jesus.
Indeed, St Paul places him among the authoritative
figures in the foundational community of Jerusalem
(Galatians 1:18-2:21). But of this rehabilitation Mark
has not a word. Why?

History and interpretation! Mark edits his picture
of Simon Peter (and of the rest of the disciples) in
order to emphasise the potential for failure endemic
in faith. Mark's disciples fail to understand Jesus, fail
to understand his destiny, fail to put behind them
pretensions to power and position and, in the end,

"they all forsook him and fled". No doubt much of this is what happened but Mark has underlined the failure and Peter is dramatised as the one whom Jesus calls Satan (Mark 8:33) and the one who denies his friend three times. Small wonder, then, that the angel at the empty tomb commanded the women,

> Go, tell his disciples and Peter, that he is going before you to Galilee; there you will see him, as he told you.
>
> Mark 16:7

Tell my disciples. And Peter. Especially Peter.

Mark is writing gospel for his time and his place. He places the failure of Simon Peter and the rest on centre-stage. Mark is saying that the story of Jesus is a story of failure, of admiring crowds in Galilee and crucifixion in Jerusalem. He is saying that failure has potential, that where there is a broken body there may be an empty tomb nearby.

Failure is gospel.

DISCUSSION SUGGESTIONS

1. Can the Church cope with failure? Can the Church cope with sin?
2. Can God cope with failure? Can God cope with sin?
3. Are all people on this planet, including Peter, saved?

THE SEVENTH STATION

Jesus Falls the Second Time

ENTRANCE:

Processional music or appropriate hymn.
Unveiling of the Cross.
Lighting of candles, use of incense, or other appropriate
acts of veneration of the Cross.

OPENING PRAYER RECITED BY ALL:

Almighty God,
be mindful,
we pray you,
of this your family,
for whose sake our Lord Jesus Christ,
when he was betrayed,
did not hesitate to undergo the agony of the Cross.
May our prayerful following in his footsteps
renew in us
our work of faith,
our labour of love,
and our steadfastness of hope.

RESPONSE:

We adore you, O Christ, and we praise you,
because by your holy Cross you have
redeemed the world.

Narrator: When they had sung a hymn, they went to the Mount of Olives. And Jesus said to them,

Jesus: You will all fall away; for it is written, 'I will strike the shepherd, and the sheep will be scattered'. But after I am raised up, I will go before you to Galilee.

Narrator: Peter said to him,

Peter: Even though they all fall away, I will not.

Narrator: And Jesus said to him,

Jesus: Truly, I say to you, this very night, before the cock crows twice, you will deny me three times.

Narrator: But he said vehemently,

Peter: If I must die with you, I will not deny you.

Narrator: And they all said the same.

COMMENTARY:

Jesus had told Peter and Andrew, and James and John to take heed, to pray, and to watch (Mark 13 *passim*). They had been clearly forewarned of the fate which awaited Jesus in Jerusalem. They had sat at table with Jesus and shared bread and wine with him.

SILENT REFLECTION

Kyrie, eleison.
                                        Kyrie, eleison.
                                        Kyrie, eleison.

READING

Narrator: They went to a place which was called Gethsemane; and Jesus said to his disciples,

Jesus: Sit here, while I pray.

Narrator: And he took with him Peter and James and John, and began to be greatly distressed and troubled. And he said to them,

Jesus: My soul is very sorrowful, even to death; remain here and watch.

Narrator: And going a little further, he fell on the ground and prayed that, if it were possible, the hour might pass from him. And he said,

Jesus: Abba, Father, all things are possible to you; remove this cup from me; yet not what I will, but what you will.

Narrator: And he came and found them sleeping, and he said to Peter,

Jesus: Simon, are you asleep? Could you not watch one hour? Watch and pray that you may not enter into temptation; the spirit indeed is willing, but the flesh is weak.

Narrator: And again he went away and prayed in the same words. And again he came and found them sleeping, for their eyes were very heavy; and they did not know what to answer him. And he came a third time, and said to them,

Jesus: Are you still sleeping and taking your rest? It is enough; the hour has come; the Son of man is betrayed into the hands of sinners. Rise, let us be going, my betrayer is at hand.

SILENT REFLECTION

HYMN: *Christe, eleison.*
                        Christe, eleison.
                        Christe, eleison.

READING

Narrator: As Peter was below in the courtyard, one of the maids of the high priest came; and seeing Peter warming himself, she looked at him, and said,

Maid: You also were with the Nazarene, Jesus.

Narrator: But he denied it, saying,

Peter: I neither know nor understand what you mean.

Narrator: And he went out into the gateway. And the maid saw him, and began to say to the bystanders,

Maid: This man is one of them.

Narrator: But again he denied it. And after a little while again the bystanders said to Peter,

Bystanders: Certainly you are one of them; for you are a Galilean.

Narrator: But he began to curse and swear,

Peter: I do not know this man of whom you speak.

Narrator: And immediately the cock crowed a second time. And Peter remembered how Jesus had said to him, "Before the cock crows twice, you will deny me three times". And he broke down and wept.

SILENT REFLECTION

HYMN: *Kyrie, eleison.*
                        Kyrie, eleison.
                        Kyrie, eleison.

PRAYERS OF INTERCESSION

LEADER: God so loved us that He gave his Son
to *carry* our sins,
to *bear* the intolerable burdens we place upon ourselves,
to *raise* us out of the terrors we create in our world.
Surely he has borne our griefs
and carried our sorrows.
Let us pray, therefore, with confidence that our hearts
may be open to the gospel of the Cross of Jesus.

1. As we follow in the footsteps of Jesus,
let us pray
that our hearts may be opened to the depth and riches
and wisdom of God's love for all peoples.

ALL: Lord, in your mercy, hear our prayer.

2. As we follow in the footsteps of Jesus,
let us pray

that we may persevere in our sufferings,
knowing that suffering produces endurance,
and endurance produces character,
and character produces hope
that does not disappoint,
because God's love has been poured into our hearts.

ALL: Lord, in your mercy, hear our prayer.

3. As we follow in the footsteps of Jesus,
let us pray
that our faith may not be compromised
by betrayal,
by self-seeking,
by weakness,
or fleeting pleasure.

ALL: Lord, in your mercy, hear our prayer.

4. As we follow in the footsteps of Jesus,
let us pray
that our hearts may be open
to God's forgiveness,
that we may not be crushed
by the burdens of our weaknesses.

ALL: Lord, in your mercy, hear our prayer.

5. Bidding Prayers from the congregation.

ALL: Almighty God,
                  be mindful,
                 we pray you,
              of this your family,
         for whose sake our Lord Jesus Christ,

when he was betrayed,
did not hesitate to undergo the agony of the Cross.
May our prayerful following in his footsteps
renew in us
our work of faith,
our labour of love,
and our steadfastness of hope.
AMEN

BLESSING:

May the God of steadfastness and encouragement grant that we may live in such harmony with one another, in accord with Jesus Christ, that together we may with one voice glorify the God and Father of our Lord Jesus Christ.

And may the blessing of Almighty God,
Father, Son, and Holy Spirit,
come down upon us,
and remain in our hearts and in our homes forever.
AMEN

ALL: We adore you, O Christ, and we praise you,
because by your holy Cross you have
redeemed the world.

RECESSIONAL HYMN:

Amazing Grace! How sweet the sound
John Newton (1725-1807)

During the hymn the Cross is covered.
All reverence the Cross and depart.

Women of Jerusalem Weep for Jesus

BACKGROUND:

All four Gospels record that women were close to Jesus. But the way women are presented in the Gospels is odd, an oddity that must be explained as each Gospel is explored.

Take St Mark. Immediately after the account of the death of Jesus and the events of that dread moment, Mark suddenly introduces a band of women:

> There were also women looking from afar, among whom were Mary Magdalene, and Mary the mother of James the younger and Joses, and Salome, who when he was in Galilee *followed* him, and *served* him; and also many other women who came up with him to Jerusalem.
>
> Mark 15:40-41

What is especially surprising about the mention of these women is that they appear out of the blue, without any obvious preparation of the reader. It is, after all, startling to discover that a celibate male teacher had been accompanied on his travels by women, some (apparently) not married, and some married, all unchaperoned.

At the beginning of St Mark's story, Jesus heals the fevered mother-in-law of Peter and immediately, we are told, she *served* them (Mark 1:29-31). It is the word "served" here which jumps off the page. When Jesus was tested in the desert by Satan, the angels *served* him (Mark 1:13). When Jesus wished to describe the nature of his own ministry of service, and to instruct the Twelve on the essence of their discipleship, this is what he says:

> You know that those who are supposed to rule over the Gentiles lord it over them, and their great men exercise authority over them. But it shall not be so among you; but whoever would be great among you must be your *servant*, and whoever would be first among you must be the slave of all. For the Son of man also came *not to be served* but *to serve*, and to give his life as a ransom for many.
>
> Mark 10:42-45

And:

> And he sat down and called the Twelve; and he said to them, "If any one would be first, he must be last of all and *the servant* of all.
>
> Mark 9:35

The women who followed Jesus and, though standing afar off, witnessed the death of Jesus and the place where he was laid, are precisely those who served him when he was in Galilee and on the journey to Jerusalem. Serving is the way of angels; serving is the way of Jesus; serving is the way of the women. The Twelve and other (men) disciples hear much about serving in Mark's Gospel. It is an essential characteristic of the Kingdom of God, of being where God's will is done on this earth as it is in heaven. Serving is what the Twelve in St Mark's Gospel never quite manage to do.

The Greek word in the Gospels for *servant* is *diakonos*. It is the ordinary word for one who waits on tables, for slave-service, generally considered demeaning and undignified. Plato, the great Greek philosopher, expressed the chattering classes' attitude toward service and serving: "How can a man be happy when he has to serve someone?" (*Gorgias* 491e). Jesus derides such superficiality. True happiness comes from the service of others. Service is next to Godliness. It is the servant who most truly mirrors God's way with the world. The Christian word "deacon" is the Greek word *diakonos*.

The serving women are there at the beginning of the work of Jesus. The serving women accompany him on the way through Galilee and onward to the fate that lies in Jerusalem. The serving women are there to watch the death of the one who said, "I am among you as one who serves" (Luke 22:27). It is, of course, to these serving women, determined to do women's work of anointing the corpse, to whom the angel announces,

> Do not be amazed; you seek Jesus of Nazareth, who was crucified. He has risen, he is not here; see the place where they laid him.
>
> Mark 16:6

Of course, the men were long gone.

104

DISCUSSION SUGGESTIONS

1. What importance (if any) should the Churches today give to the fact that, in St Mark's Gospel, women follow Jesus, serve him, and, unlike the Twelve (Peter, James, John and the rest), witness the death of Jesus and his burial and, surprisingly, are the sole witnesses to the empty tomb and the angel's message?

2. In St Paul's Letter to the Romans (16:1), the great apostle writes, "I commend to you our sister Phoebe, a *deacon* of the church at Cenchreae". Should we ignore this?

3. The women entered into the suffering of Jesus. How could Christians of today join themselves to the suffering and death of Jesus?

Women of Jerusalem Weep for Jesus

ENTRANCE:

Processional music or appropriate hymn.
Unveiling of the Cross.
Lighting of candles, use of incense, or other appropriate
acts of veneration of the Cross.

OPENING PRAYER RECITED BY ALL:

Almighty God,
be mindful,
we pray you,
of this your family,
for whose sake our Lord Jesus Christ,
when he was betrayed,
did not hesitate to undergo the agony of the Cross.
May our prayerful following in his footsteps
renew in us
our work of faith,
our labour of love,
and our steadfastness of hope.

RESPONSE:

We adore you, O Christ, and we praise you,
because by your holy Cross you have
redeemed the world.

A READING FROM PSALM 69
Psalm 69:16-21

READER: Answer me, O LORD,
for your steadfast love is good;
according to your abundant mercy,
turn to me.

Do not hide your face from your servant,
for I am in distress —
make haste to answer me.
Draw near to me, redeem me,
set me free because of my enemies.

You know the insults I receive,
and my shame and dishonour;
my foes are all known to you.
Insults have broken my heart,
so that I am in despair.

I looked for pity,
but there was none;
I looked for comforters,
but I found none.
They gave me poison for my food
and vinegar to drink.

COMMENTARY:

In St Mark's Gospel, Jesus dies alone, among his
enemies, with no human kindness to soften the

inexorable brutality. Even at the moment of death, there is no respite, only an agonising cry: "My God, my God, why have you forsaken me?" (Mark 14: 34). Did God answer the agony of Jesus, did God hear his prayer?

SILENT REFLECTION

A READING FROM THE PROPHET ISAIAH
Isaiah 53:2-6

READER: He had no form or comeliness
that we should look at him,
no beauty that we should desire him.

[Sing]
O Lord, hear our prayer,
O Lord, hear our prayer.
When we call, answer us.
O Lord, hear our prayer,
O Lord, hear our prayer.
Come and listen to us.
(Taizé Chant)

He was despised,
rejected by men and women,
a man of sorrows, acquainted with grief.
He was despised
as one from whom people hide their faces
and we esteemed him not.

O Lord, hear our prayer,
O Lord, hear our prayer.
When we call, answer us.
O Lord, hear our prayer,
O Lord, hear our prayer.
Come and listen to us.

Surely he has borne our griefs
and carried our sorrows;
yet we esteemed him stricken,
smitten by God, afflicted.

O Lord, hear our prayer,
O Lord, hear our prayer.
When we call, answer us.
O Lord, hear our prayer,
O Lord, hear our prayer.
Come and listen to us.

He was wounded for our transgressions,
he was bruised for our iniquities;
upon him was the punishment
that made us whole,
and by his bruises we are healed.

O Lord, hear our prayer,
O Lord, hear our prayer.
When we call, answer us.
O Lord, hear our prayer,
O Lord, hear our prayer.
Come and listen to us.

All of us, like sheep, had gone astray;
we turned, each of us, to our own way.
But the LORD laid on him
the iniquity of us all.

O Lord, hear our prayer,
O Lord, hear our prayer.
When we call, answer us.
O Lord, hear our prayer,
O Lord, hear our prayer.
Come and listen to us.

PRAYERS OF INTERCESSION

LEADER: God so loved us that He gave his Son
to *carry* our sins,
to *bear* the intolerable burdens we place upon ourselves,
to *raise* us out of the terrors we create in our world.
Surely he has borne our griefs and carried our sorrows.
Let us pray, therefore, with confidence that our hearts
may be open to the gospel of the Cross of Jesus.

1. As we follow in the footsteps of Jesus,
let us pray
that our hearts may be opened to the depth and riches
and wisdom of God's love for all peoples.

ALL: Lord, in your mercy, hear our prayer.

2. As we follow in the footsteps of Jesus,
let us pray
that we may persevere in our sufferings,

knowing that suffering produces endurance,
and endurance produces character,
and character produces hope
that does not disappoint,
because God's love has been poured into our hearts.

ALL: Lord, in your mercy, hear our prayer.

3. As we follow in the footsteps of Jesus,
let us pray
that, like the women who openly mourned for him,
we may seek to understand
that Jesus bore our weaknesses, our failings and our sins.

ALL: Lord, in your mercy, hear our prayer.

4. As we follow in the footsteps of Jesus,
let us pray
that our hearts may be open
to all who suffer
from violence,
from injustice,
and from all human iniquity.

ALL: Lord, in your mercy, hear our prayer.

5. Bidding Prayers from the congregation.

ALL: Almighty God,
                       be mindful,
                    we pray you,
                 of this your family,
           for whose sake our Lord Jesus Christ,
                when he was betrayed,
       did not hesitate to undergo the agony of the Cross.

May our prayerful following in his footsteps
renew in us
our work of faith,
our labour of love,
and our steadfastness of hope.

AMEN.

BLESSING:

May the God of steadfastness and encouragement
grant us to live in such harmony with one another,
in accord with Jesus Christ, that together we may
with one voice glorify the God and Father of our
Lord Jesus Christ.

And may the blessing of Almighty God,
Father, Son, and Holy Spirit,
come down upon us,
and remain in our hearts and in our homes forever.

AMEN.

ALL: We adore you, O Christ, and we praise you,
because by your holy Cross you have
redeemed the world.

RECESSIONAL HYMN:

Soul of my Saviour.
Pope John XII (1249-1334)

During the hymn the Cross is covered.
All reverence the Cross and depart.

Jesus Falls the Third Time

BACKGROUND:

Jesus drew large crowds. Of course, what constitutes a large crowd in a small country with a sparse population is a moot point. But all the Gospels and other commentators, such as the Jewish historian, Josephus, and the Roman historian, Tacitus, both first-century figures, record that Jesus attracted crowds. Gospel readers often neglect the crowds as no more than a background to the mighty words and deeds of Jesus. But the crowd is a real actor in the drama and must not be relegated to the wings.

St Mark draws a line between the crowds and the authorities, on the one hand, and between the crowds and the Twelve and disciples, on the other. The crowds are not sinners (whoever they are), not tax collectors, not the well-to-do, nor, exclusively, the ne'er-do-well.

Jesus *taught* the crowds:

> He went out again beside the sea; and the crowd gathered about him, and he *taught* them.
>
> Mark 2:13

> Again he began to teach beside the sea. And a very large crowd gathered about him, so that he got into a boat and sat in it on the sea; and the

113

whole crowd was beside the sea on the land.
And he *taught* them many things in parables…

Mark 4:1-2

And he called the crowd to him again, and said
to them, "*Hear* me, all of you, and *understand*…

Mark 7:14

And he left there and went to the region of
Judea and beyond the Jordan, and the crowds
gathered
to him again; and again, as his custom was, he
taught them.

Mark 10:1

Jesus *healed* the sick brought to him by the crowds:

That evening, at sundown, they brought to him
all who were sick or possessed with demons.
And the whole city was gathered together at the
door. And he *healed* many who were sick with
various diseases, and cast out many demons…

Mark 1:32-34

And a great crowd followed him and thronged
about him. And there was a woman who had
a flow of blood for twelve years and she had
endured so much … be healed of your disease.

Mark 5:24

And when [Jesus and Peter and James and John]
came to the disciples, they saw a great crowd
about them, and scribes arguing with them. And

immediately all the crowd, when they saw him,
were greatly amazed, and ran up to him and
greeted him. And he asked them. "What are you
discussing with them?" And one of the crowd
answered him, "Teacher, I brought my son to
you, for he has a dumb spirit ...

Mark 9:14-16

And, above all, in Mark's view, the compassion of
Jesus for the crowds moved him to *feed* them:

As he landed he saw a great crowd, and he had
compassion on them, because they were like
sheep without a shepherd; and he began to *teach*
them many things. And when it grew late, his
disciples came to him and said, "This is a lonely
place, and the hour is now late; send them away,
to go into the country and villages around about
to buy themselves something to eat". But he
answered them, "You give them something to
eat".

Mark 6:34-37

In those days, when again a great crowd had
gathered, and they had nothing to eat, he called
his disciples to him, and said to them, "I have
compassion on the crowd, because they have
been with me now three days, and have nothing
to eat; and if I send them away hungry to their
homes, they will faint on the way; and some of
them have come a long way".

Mark 8:1-3

Welcoming, teaching, healing and *feeding*. No wonder that "The great crowd heard him gladly" (Mark 12:37).

And the next thing we hear of the crowd is that it is demanding the release of the rebel and murderer Barabbas and crying for the blood of Jesus of Nazareth: *Crucify him! Crucify him!* (Mark 15:6-15).

History and interpretation. Of course, from the point of view of history, it would be wrong to assume that the same crowd followed Jesus everywhere. It would be misguided to believe that the crowd which gathered in Capernaum was the same which assembled in Jerusalem, eighty miles away. It would, indeed, be foolhardy to suppose that the people (not "the crowd") who paraded on Palm Sunday made up the crowd who cried "Crucify him" on Good Friday, as naive sermons frequently do.

History and interpretation. But, from the point of view of interpretation, for Mark the crowd is the anonymous multitude from whom disciples may emerge but who, having received *teaching, healing* and *feeding* from Jesus, may, without thanks, wither away, like the seed which fell on stony ground (Mark 4: 1-6).

In other words, Mark's crowd is ominously like ourselves. After all we have heard, after all we have seen, after all the care and love, we know that we can fall – even three times.

DISCUSSION SUGGESTIONS

1. Even though his efforts were not crowned with success, Jesus welcomed crowds of people, talked with them, healed their sick, and fed them. What lessons ought the Churches to learn from Jesus about their approach to people in our day and age?
2. Do people have to come and join the Church before the Church does anything for them?
3. When we fall, how does God pick us up?

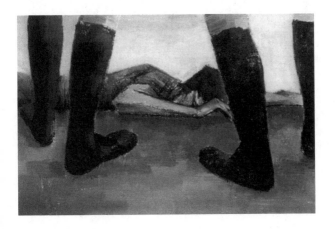

Jesus Falls the Third Time

ENTRANCE:

Processional music or appropriate hymn.
Unveiling of the Cross.
Lighting of candles, use of incense, or other appropriate
acts of veneration of the Cross.

OPENING PRAYER RECITED BY ALL:

Almighty God,
be mindful,
we pray you,
of this your family,
for whose sake our Lord Jesus Christ,
when he was betrayed,
did not hesitate to undergo the agony of the Cross.
May our prayerful following in his footsteps
renew in us
our work of faith,
our labour of love,
and our steadfastness of hope.

RESPONSE:

We adore you, O Christ, and we praise you,
because by your holy Cross you have
redeemed the world.

Narrator: As soon as it was morning the chief priests, with the elders and the scribes, and the whole council, held a consultation; and they bound Jesus and led him away and delivered him to Pilate. And Pilate asked him,

Pilate: Are you the King of the Jews?

Narrator: And he answered him,

Jesus: You have said so.

Narrator: And the chief priests accused him of many things. And Pilate asked him,

Pilate: Have you no answer to make? See how many charges they bring against you.

Narrator: But Jesus made no further answer, so that Pilate wondered. Now at the feast he used to release for them one prisoner for whom they asked. And among the rebels in prison, who had committed murder in the uprising, there was a man called Barabbas. And the crowd came up and began to ask Pilate to do for them as was his custom. And he answered them,

Pilate: Do you want me to release to you the King of the Jews?

Narrator: For he perceived that it was out of envy that the chief priests had handed him over. But the chief priests stirred up the crowd to have him release for them Barabbas instead. And Pilate again said to them,

Pilate: Then what shall I do with the man whom you call King of the Jews?

Narrator: And they cried out again,

Crowd: Crucify him!

Narrator: And Pilate said to them,

Pilate: Why? What evil has he done?

Narrator: But they shouted all the more,

Crowd: Crucify him!

Narrator: So Pilate, wishing to satisfy the crowd, released for them Barabbas and having scourged Jesus, he handed him over to be crucified.

COMMENTARY:

When Jesus fed the great crowd of five thousand, all were *satisfied* with what Jesus had made for them out of the five loaves and two fish (Mark 6:42). And when he fed the great crowd of four thousand with but seven loaves, all were satisfied (Mark 8:8). Now it is Pilate's turn to *satisfy* the hungry crowd. And he released for them Barabbas; and having scourged Jesus, he handed him over to be crucified.

SILENT REFLECTION

PRAYERS OF INTERCESSION

LEADER: God so loved us that He gave his Son to *carry* our sins,

to *bear* the intolerable burdens we place upon ourselves,
to *raise* us out of the terrors we create in our world.
Surely he has borne our griefs
and carried our sorrows.
Let us pray, therefore, with confidence that our hearts
may be open to the gospel of the Cross of Jesus.

1. As we follow in the footsteps of Jesus,
let us pray
that our hearts may be opened to the depth and riches
and wisdom of God's love for all peoples.

ALL: Lord, in your mercy, hear our prayer.

2. As we follow in the footsteps of Jesus,
let us pray
that we remain faithful,
that we listen with open ears,
that we learn with loving hearts,
and that we be satisfied with what the Lord provides.

ALL: Lord, in your mercy, hear our prayer.

3. As we follow in the footsteps of Jesus,
let us pray
that we may not be embarrassed into denial,
coerced into popular choices,
and deluded by false hopes.

ALL: Lord, in your mercy, hear our prayer.

4. As we follow in the footsteps of Jesus,
let us pray that all who have fallen into despair
and who are bereft of hope
may be encouraged by the steadfastness of God's love
revealed in the suffering of his Son.

ALL: Lord, in your mercy, hear our prayer.

5. Bidding Prayers from the congregation.

ALL: Almighty God,
                        be mindful,
                        we pray you,
                    of this your family,
            for whose sake our Lord Jesus Christ,
                    when he was betrayed,
        did not hesitate to undergo the agony of the Cross.
            May our prayerful following in his footsteps
                        renew in us
                      our work of faith,
                    our labour of love,
              and our steadfastness of hope.
                        AMEN.

BLESSING:

May the God of steadfastness and encouragement grant
us to live in such harmony with one another, in accord
with Jesus Christ, that together we may with one
voice glorify the God and Father of our Lord Jesus
Christ.

And may the blessing of Almighty God,
Father, Son, and Holy Spirit,
come down upon us,
and remain in our hearts and in our homes forever.
                                            AMEN.

ALL: We adore you, O Christ, and we praise you,
            because by your holy Cross you have
                    redeemed the world.

Keep in mind that Jesus Christ
Lucien Deiss

During the hymn the Cross is covered.
All reverence the Cross and depart.

Jesus is Stripped of His Garments

BACKGROUND:

According to St Mark, after the mockery with the purple cloak and the crown of thorns (Mark 15:16-19), the soldiers " stripped him of the purple cloak and put his own clothes on him and led him out to crucify him" (Mark 15:20). There are interesting and not unimportant issues lurking in these snippets of information.

First, in St John's Gospel, the soldiers place a crown of thorns on the head of Jesus and they dress him in a purple robe (John 19:1-3). Then Pilate brings Jesus out before "the chief priests and the officers" and, the writer emphasises, still "wearing the crown of thorns and the purple robe" (John 19:4-5). Pilate proclaims his famous line, *Ecce homo! Behold, the man!* The King of the Jews is presented in royal robes. Indeed, it would appear that Jesus goes out carrying his own cross still dressed in the crown and purple robe. Jesus, in John's perspective, goes to the cross as to a throne and the King mounts the cross to reign. Interpretation is considerably ahead of history in much of the Fourth Gospel.

Secondly, what we know about crucifixion forces us to the conclusion that Jesus was stripped naked, dragged naked through the streets, flogged along the way, and, still naked, nailed to the cross. That criminals were stripped completely naked and dragged to the place of execution was part of the punishment, part of the humiliation. Ancient writers, such as Dionysius of Halicarnassus and Valerius Maximus, provide evidence for what was routine practice. Josephus records that Cherea and other nobles involved in the assassination of the Roman emperor Gaius Caligula in 41 AD. were stripped naked before being led to execution. The earliest portrayals of the crucifixion of Jesus (mainly carved gemstones) – only about a half-dozen between the second to the fifth century survive – depict a nude figure. In the late second century, Melito of Sardis laments that Jesus was crucified "with his body naked and not even deemed worthy of clothing that it might not be seen". He supposes that the "day darkened in order that he might be hidden who was stripped naked on the cross". Yet the popular but fictional Acts of Pilate has this to say:

> And Jesus went out from the praetorium, and the two malefactors with him. And when they came to the place, they stripped him and girded him with a linen cloth [Latin, *subligaculum* = a loincloth] and put a crown of thorns on his head.
>
> Acts of Pilate 10:1

And, indeed, it has been suggested that Roman authority bowed to Jewish abhorrence of nudity and allowed a loincloth. However, Roman magnanimity cannot be assumed and certainly not in the case of a criminal whose alleged targets were the power bases underlying the authority of Pilate and Caiaphas. Jesus, we can be sure, was naked as he stumbled through the streets of Jerusalem and as he hung on the cross.

Thirdly, therefore, why do the Gospels have so much to say about his garments? All four Gospels indicate that his garments were divided among the execution detail and that drawing lots (throwing dice) decided who got what. But if Jesus was naked…

The answer lies in Psalm 22 and in the efforts of the first Christians firmly to discover every detail of the life of Jesus, but especially his suffering and death, in their Holy Scriptures, in their Bible. If the death of Jesus was God's will, then, since Jesus is God's Son, God's holy word must, in some fashion, signal that momentous event. Psalm 22 is the angry prayer of a soul in distress, beset by enemies and in despair of any help from God. Read the following quotations and then confront an inevitable question:

> My God, my God, why have you forsaken me?
> Why are you so far from helping me,
> from the words of my groaning?
> O my God, I cry by day,
> but you do not answer,
> and by night,
> but find no rest.
> (Verses 1-2)

> But I am a worm, and no man;
> scorned by men,
> and despised by the people.
> All who see me mock at me,

> they make mouths at me,
> they wag their heads;
> "He committed his cause to the Lord!
> Let him deliver him,
> let him [God] rescue him,
> for he [God] delights in him."
> (Verses 6-8)

> I am poured out like water,
> and all my bones are out of joint;
> my heart is like wax,
> it is melted within my breast;
> my strength is dried up like a potsherd,
> and my tongue cleaves to my jaws;
> thou dost lay me in the dust of death.
> Yea, dogs are round about me;
> a company of evildoers encircle me;
> they have pierced my hands and my feet –
> they stare and gloat over me;
> they divide my garments among them,
> and for my raiment they cast lots.
> (Verses 14-18)

The question is easily stated and immensely difficult to answer with entire satisfaction:

• Did the Christian desire to interpret the inner meaning of what they believed was God's agenda in the sordid story of the routine crucifixion of Jesus of Nazareth occasionally so varnish the facts that they, the facts, are too buried to be recoverable?

• Or, to cut the cackle and come to the horses, did they make things up, now and again?

DISCUSSION SUGGESTIONS

1. We must be alert to the fact that the gospel-makers sometimes presented the truths which they sought to convey in ways that we may find disturbing. Poetry, narrative fiction, creative quotation – all are put at the service of proclaiming who Jesus is and what he did. Do you find it difficult to come to terms with this? And, if so, why?

2. Do the delicacies of Christian art, and even modesty, disguise the horrors of crucifixion, and anaesthetise us from the realities of the suffering of its victims?

3. Metaphorically speaking, do our Churches need to strip off the layers of garments which we have acquired over the centuries? And, to change the metaphor, how do we avoid throwing out the baby with the bath water?

Jesus is Stripped of His Garments

ENTRANCE:

Processional music or appropriate hymn.
Unveiling of the Cross.
Lighting of candles, use of incense, or other appropriate
acts of veneration of the Cross.

OPENING PRAYER RECITED BY ALL:

Almighty God,
be mindful,
we pray you,
of this your family,
for whose sake our Lord Jesus Christ,
when he was betrayed,
did not hesitate to undergo the agony of the Cross.
May our prayerful following in his footsteps
renew in us
our work of faith,
our labour of love,
and our steadfastness of hope.

RESPONSE:

We adore you, O Christ, and we praise you,
because by your holy Cross you have
redeemed the world.

Narrator: The soldiers led him away inside the palace (that is, the praetorium); and they called together the whole battalion. And they clothed him in a purple cloak, and plaiting a crown of thorns they put it on him. And they began to salute him, "Hail, King of the Jews!" And they struck his head with a reed, they spat upon him, and they knelt down in homage to him. And when they had mocked him, they stripped him of the purple cloak, and put his own clothes on him. And they led him out to crucify him.

SILENT REFLECTION

HYMN: *Were you there when they crucified my Lord?*
Traditional American Spiritual

Were you there when they crucified my Lord?
Were you there when they crucified my Lord?
Oh sometimes it causes me to tremble, tremble, tremble.
Were you there when they crucified my Lord?

Were you there when they stripped him of his crown?
Were you there when they stripped him of his crown?
Oh sometimes it causes me to tremble, tremble, tremble.
Were you there when they stripped him of his crown?

Narrator: They led him out to crucify him. And they compelled a passer-by, Simon of Cyrene, who was coming in from the country, the father of Alexander and Rufus, to carry his cross. They brought him to the place called Golgotha (which means The Place of the Skull). And they offered him wine mingled with myrrh; but he did not drink it. And they crucified him, and divided his garments among them, casting lots for them, to decide what each should take.

SILENT REFLECTION

HYMN:

Were you there when they dragged him through the streets?
Were you there when they dragged him through the streets?
Oh sometimes it causes me to tremble, tremble, tremble.
Were you there when they dragged him through the streets?

Were you there when they gave him wine and myrrh?
Were you there when they gave him wine and myrrh?
Oh sometimes it causes me to tremble, tremble, tremble.
Were you there when they gave him wine and myrrh?

Narrator: It was the third hour when they crucified him. And the inscription of the charge against him read, "The King of the Jews". And with him they crucified two robbers, one on his right and one on his left. And those who passed by derided him, wagging their heads, and saying, "Aha! You would destroy the temple and build it in three days, save yourself, and come down from the cross!" So also the chief priests mocked him to one another with the scribes, saying, "He saved others; he cannot save himself. Let the Messiah, the King of Israel, come down now from the cross, that we may see and believe." Those who were crucified with him also reviled him.

SILENT REFLECTION

HYMN:

> *Were you there when they crucified my Lord?*
> *Were you there when they crucified my Lord?*
> *Oh sometimes it causes me to tremble, tremble, tremble*
> *Were you there when they crucified my Lord?*
>
> *Were you there when they nailed him to a tree?*
> *Were you there when they nailed him to a tree?*
> *Oh sometimes it causes me to tremble, tremble, tremble.*
> *Were you there when they nailed him to a tree?*
>
> *Were you there when they crucified my Lord?*
> *Were you there when they crucified my Lord?*
> *Oh sometimes it causes me to tremble, tremble, tremble.*
> *Were you there when they crucified my Lord?*

PRAYERS OF INTERCESSION

LEADER: God so loved us that He gave his Son
to *carry* our sins,
to *bear* the intolerable burdens we place upon ourselves,
to *raise* us out of the terrors we create in our world.
Surely he has borne our griefs
and carried our sorrows.

Let us pray, therefore, with confidence that our hearts may be open to the gospel of the Cross of Jesus.

1. As we follow in the footsteps of Jesus,
let us pray
that our hearts may be opened to the depth and riches
and wisdom of God's love for all peoples.

ALL: Lord, in your mercy, hear our prayer.

2. As we follow in the footsteps of Jesus,
let us pray
that we rejoice in hope,
be patient in tribulation,
and constant in prayer.

ALL: Lord, in your mercy, hear our prayer.

3. As we follow in the footsteps of Jesus,
let us pray
that we
bless those who deride us,
rejoice with those who rejoice,
weep with those who weep.

ALL: Lord, in your mercy, hear our prayer.

4. As we follow in the footsteps of Jesus,
let us pray
that we repay no one evil for evil,
but take thought for what is good;
that we live in harmony with one another
and in peace with all people.

ALL: Lord, in your mercy, hear our prayer.

5. Bidding Prayers from the congregation.

ALL: Almighty God,
                        be mindful,
                        we pray you,
                      of this your family,
            for whose sake our Lord Jesus Christ,
                    when he was betrayed,
      did not hesitate to undergo the agony of the Cross.
        May our prayerful following in his footsteps
                        renew in us
                      our work of faith,
                      our labour of love,
              and our steadfastness of hope.
                          AMEN.

BLESSING:

May the God of steadfastness and encouragement
grant us to live in such harmony with one another,
in accord with Jesus Christ, that together we may
with one voice glorify the God and Father of our
Lord Jesus Christ.

And may the blessing of Almighty God,
Father, Son, and Holy Spirit,
come down upon us,
and remain in our hearts and in our homes forever.
                                                AMEN.

ALL: We adore you, O Christ, and we praise you,
        because by your holy Cross you have
                redeemed the world.

Lord, make me an instrument of thy peace.
Based on a prayer mistakenly ascribed to St Francis

During the hymn the Cross is covered.
All reverence the Cross and depart.

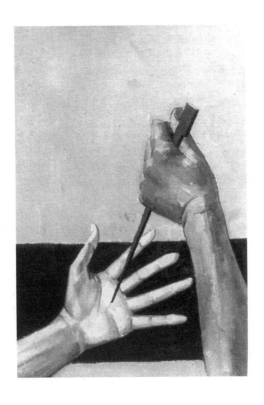

Jesus is Nailed to the Cross

BACKGROUND:

In June, 1968, Vassilios Tzaferis, of the Israel Antiquities Authority, was excavating several burial caves in the northern Jerusalem suburb of Givat Hamivtar. In one rock-hewn tomb he found eight ossuaries (bone boxes), one of which contained the skeletal remains of two men and a young child. One of the men and the child were named Yehohanan. The man had been crucified.

Yehohanan was 5 feet 5 inches tall and about twenty years old. His right heel bone had been pierced by a four-and-a-half inch nail at whose head was still attached a small olivewood washer. The man's legs seem to have straddled the upright of his cross (an old stripped olive tree?), so that his feet were nailed to either side of it, not the front. Each nail was hammered first through the wooden washer, then through the heel bone, and so into the cross or tree. The washer prevented the crucified victim from pulling his feet free of the nail. Because the nail bent when it was hammered home and could not be easily extracted, the ankle, nail and washer remained together when the body was taken down and buried. Sometime later the bones of the victim were deposited in an ossuary with the heel, nail and wooden washer still connected together. The arms were tied, not nailed, to the crossbeam, as the wrist bones were undamaged. The leg bones appear to have been broken when the bones were deposited in the ossuary but not deliberately broken when Yehohanan was dying on the cross.

The remains of this victim who met his death within a few years of the crucifixion of Jesus shed much light on how Jesus died. Jesus would have carried the crossbeam and, on arrival at Golgotha, he would have been hoisted on to a vertical post or tree. He may well have been nailed to the crossbeam but through the wrists, not the hands. His legs would have been straddled around the upright and nailed to it through his ankles. There might have been a *suppedaneum*, a footrest or similar support, not as an act of mercy but to enable the victim to breathe by lifting himself. In this way, suffering would last longer but breaking the legs would curtail the agony if, for whatever reason, the execution detail decided to end matters.

Christian art and commentators on the details of crucifixion may reflect local practices and, perhaps, theological speculation. For example, a fifth-century ivory box in the British Museum and a wooden door panel in St Sabina's in Rome, portray Jesus on the cross but show no nails in the feet. In the Russian cross there is always a short crossbeam traversing the upright near the bottom which provided a seat to take the weight of the victim and thus prolong the suffering. Artistic licence and theological speculation explain many of the different ways in which the dying Jesus has been depicted from the outlandish speculation of Justin Martyr in the second century to the sentimental tosh of Salvador Dali in the twentieth.

Meditation, reflection and prayer have, thank God, made blessings: *The Dream of the Rood*, Michelangelo's *Pieta* and, of course, *The Gospel according to Saint Mark*.

Thousands upon thousands of people were crucified in the ancient world. Of them there is no archaeological trace except the bones of the young man from Jerusalem. Victims of crucifixion were not given back to their families for burial. That was part, a devastating part, of the humiliation and punishment. They were left on the cross to rot, with no public mourning, no proper burial, no lying with one's ancestors in the family grave. As the poet Horace observes, those who hung on the cross fed the crows (Horace, *Epistle* 1.16.48). So why was there an exception made in the case of Yehohanan? And why, in the case of the man from Nazareth?

DISCUSSION SUGGESTIONS

1. When St Paul sought to summarise all that God had done in the life and death of Jesus of Nazareth, he said,

   WE PREACH CHRIST CRUCIFIED!

   (First Letter to the Corinthians 1:23)

   What do we preach?

2. The Church has not died. The Church is not risen. It is nailed to the cross of Jesus. How should this realisation affect the way Christians live in a world of war, injustice, poverty and starvation?

3. Why do so many people wear crosses?

Jesus is Nailed to the Cross

ENTRANCE:

Processional music or appropriate hymn.
Unveiling of the Cross.
Lighting of candles, use of incense, or other appropriate
acts of veneration of the Cross.

OPENING PRAYER RECITED BY ALL:

Almighty God,
be mindful,
we pray you,
of this your family,
for whose sake our Lord Jesus Christ,
when he was betrayed,
did not hesitate to undergo the agony of the Cross.
May our prayerful following in his footsteps
renew in us
our work of faith,
our labour of love,
and our steadfastness of hope.

RESPONSE:

We adore you, O Christ, and we praise you,
because by your holy Cross you have
redeemed the world.

A LITANY OF CRUCIFIXION

LEADER: For the word of the cross
            is folly to those who are perishing,
            but to us who are being saved,
            it is the power of God.
            For it is written,
        "I will destroy the wisdom of the wise,
   and the cleverness of the clever, I will thwart."
            Where is the wise man?
            Where is the scribe?
        Where is the debater of this age?
   Has not God made foolish the wisdom of this world?
            1 Corinthians 1:18-20

RESPONSE: *Christus vincit!*
                Christus regnat!
             Christus, Christus imperat!

LEADER: We preach Christ crucified...
            Christ the power of God
            and the wisdom of God.
            For the foolishness of God
            is wiser than men,
            and the weakness of God
            is stronger than men.
            1 Corinthians 1:23-25

RESPONSE: *Christus vincit!*
                Christus regnat!
             Christus, Christus imperat!

LEADER:

We impart a secret and hidden wisdom from God,
which God decreed before the ages for our
glorification.
None of the rulers of this age understood this
for if they had,
they would not have crucified the Lord of glory.
But it is written,
"No eye has seen,
nor ear heard,
nor the heart of man conceived,
what God has prepared for those who love him."

1 Corinthians 2:7-9

RESPONSE:
Christus vincit!
Christus regnat!
Christus, Christus imperat!

LEADER: [Christ] is not weak in dealing with you,
but is powerful in you.
For he was crucified in weakness,
but lives by the power of God.

2 Corinthians 13:3-4

RESPONSE:
Christus vincit!
Christus regnat!
Christus, Christus imperat!

LEADER: Far be it from me to glory
except in the cross of our Lord Jesus Christ,
by which the world has been crucified to me,
and I to the world.

Galatians 6:14

RESPONSE: *Christus vincit!*
                        Christus regnat!
                        Christus, Christus imperat!

LEADER: I have been crucified with Christ;
                        it is no longer I who live,
                        but Christ who lives in me;
                        and the life I now live in the flesh
                        I live by faith in the Son of God,
                        who loved me
                        and gave himself up for me.
                        Galatians 2:20

RESPONSE: *Christus vincit!*
                        Christus regnat!
                        Christus, Christus imperat!

LEADER: For if we have been united with him
                        in a death like his,
                        we shall certainly be united with him
                        in a resurrection like his.
        We know that our old self was crucified with him
                so that the sinful body might be destroyed,
                        and we might no longer be enslaved to sin.
                        For he who has died is freed from sin.
                        But if we have died with Christ,
                        we believe that we shall also live with him.
                        Romans 6: 5-8

RESPONSE: *Christus vincit!*
                        Christus regnat!
                        Christus, Christus imperat!

LEADER: The fruit of the Spirit
                           is
                         love,
                         joy,
                        peace,
                       patience,
                       kindness,
                       goodness,
                      faithfulness,
                      gentleness,
                      self-control.
              Against such there is no law.
        And those who belong to Christ [Jesus]
have crucified the flesh with its passions and desires.
            If we live by the Spirit,
            let us walk by the Spirit.
                   Galatians 5:22-25

RESPONSE: *Christus vincit!*
                     Christus regnat!
            Christus, Christus imperat!

PRAYERS OF INTERCESSION

LEADER: God so loved us that He gave his Son
to *carry* our sins,
to *bear* the intolerable burdens we place upon ourselves,
to *raise* us out of the terrors we create in our world.
Surely he has borne our griefs
and carried our sorrows.
Let us pray, therefore, with confidence that our hearts
may be open to the gospel of the Cross of Jesus.

1. As we follow in the footsteps of Jesus,
let us pray
that our hearts may be opened to the depth and riches
and wisdom of God's love for all peoples.

ALL: Lord, in your mercy, hear our prayer.

2. As we follow in the footsteps of Jesus,
let us pray
that we rejoice in hope,
be patient in tribulation,
and constant in prayer.

ALL: Lord, in your mercy, hear our prayer.

3. As we follow in the footsteps of Jesus,
let us pray
that we do not lose heart,
not grow weary in well-doing
and, as we have opportunity,
to do good to all people.

ALL: Lord, in your mercy, hear our prayer.

4. As we follow in the footsteps of Jesus,
let us pray
that we put on the armour of God,
that we may be able to withstand evil,
strong in the Lord,
and ready for every good work.

ALL: Lord, in your mercy, hear our prayer.

5. Bidding Prayers from the congregation.

ALL: Almighty God,
                       be mindful,
                       we pray you,
                    of this your family,

for whose sake our Lord Jesus Christ,
when he was betrayed,
did not hesitate to undergo the agony of the Cross.
May our prayerful following in his footsteps
renew in us
our work of faith,
our labour of love,
and our steadfastness of hope.
AMEN.

BLESSING:

May the God of steadfastness and encouragement
grant us to live in such harmony with one another,
in accord with Jesus Christ, that together we may
with one voice glorify the God and Father of our
Lord Jesus Christ.

And may the blessing of Almighty God,
Father, Son, and Holy Spirit,
come down upon us,
and remain in our hearts and in our homes forever.
AMEN.

ALL: We adore you, O Christ, and we praise you,
because by your holy Cross you have
redeemed the world.

RECESSIONAL HYMN:

Sweet heart of Jesus
Traditional Hymn

During the hymn the Cross is covered.
All reverence the Cross and depart.

Jesus Dies on the Cross

BACKGROUND:

The death of Jesus was the most significant event in human history. Whatever ones perspective, whether one accepts Christian claims, whether one rejects Christian claims, whether one is entirely indifferent to any claims made about Jesus, his death has affected human history so profoundly that even people who have never heard his name are influenced by his presence. However one may judge its responsibility for good or evil in human history, Christianity has had a most profound influence on this planet.

All the more reason, therefore, to wonder at the brevity of the accounts of the actual death which brought this influence to bear on human history. Consider what is written in the four Gospels:

Mark: *My God, my God why have you forsaken me?*
Matthew: *My God, my God, why have you forsaken me?*
Luke: *Father, into your hands I commend my spirit!*
John: *It is accomplished!*

Did Jesus die screaming that God had abandoned him? Or did he die with a quiet prayer, commending his soul to God, knowing that he had fulfilled his life's work? The careful reader will want to ask why the Mother of Jesus is present in one Gospel and not four, why two others were crucified alongside Jesus in all Gospels but Luke alone records that one prayed to his fellow victim? Why does Luke (lamely?) record that "acquaintances" of Jesus stood at a distance but fails to name them? Why do we hear so many words from mocking crowds, chief priests and scribes, passers-by, bystanders, the people, the soldiers, the centurion, the criminals, and so little from the man himself?

Consider, too, the brief notices of the moment of death:

Mark: *But Jesus, letting out a loud cry, expired* (15:37).
Matthew: *But Jesus, again crying out with a loud voice, let go the spirit* (27: 50).
Luke: *Then Jesus, crying with a loud voice, said, "Father, into your hands I commit my spirit!" But, having said this, he expired* (23:46).
John: *When Jesus had received the vinegar, he said, "It is accomplished"; and, having bowed his head, he gave up his spirit* (19:30).

These statements, written by people who believed that they were recording the last moment of the Son of God, raise a host of questions. First, when we put these statements into their context in each Gospel, we notice that it is the events surrounding the death which are of most concern to the writers. Secondly, the events accompanying the death of Jesus are not the same in each Gospel and, indeed, are contradictory. On the one hand, Mark narrates that the women were "looking on from afar" (Mark 15:40), while, on the other hand, John records that "the mother of

Jesus, and his mother's sister, Mary the wife of Clopas, and Mary Magdalene", were "standing by the cross", within hearing distance of the dying man (John19:25-27). Luke tells us that "all his acquaintances and the women who had followed him from Galilee stood afar off and saw these things" (Luke 23:49). Matthew agrees that the women were "looking from afar" (Matthew 27:55). Why don't the Gospels agree on who saw him die?

The truth of the matter is that the people who wrote the Gospels were not there. There are two reasons (at least) for this statement and there is one important conclusion (at least) to be drawn.

That the writers of our Gospels were not present is obvious from the fact that their accounts are so contradictory in detail (but not in the broad sweep of events) that it is impossible to believe that they were eye witnesses, no matter how much one allows for divergent reports by witnesses to the same event.

Secondly, to insist that each Gospel gives an un-varnished account of the death of Jesus is to miss the relationship between history and interpretation. Take a very simple phrase. Jesus uttered "a loud cry". There is, surely, nothing implausible about a death rattle from a dying man. But are Mark and Matthew simply noting an historical detail? Both writers refer to the loud cry *twice* (Mark 15:34 and 37; Matthew 27:46 and 50), thus emphasising the point. If we link the loud cry with the elements of darkness, earthquakes, and bodies of the saints coming out of the tombs, we are confronted with the kind of incidents and language

which the Bible, and early Christians, used to imagine
the "end of the world". Consider the following:

And the LORD *roars* from Zion,
and *utters his voice* from Jerusalem,
and *the heavens and the earth shake.*
But the LORD is a refuge to his people,
a stronghold to the people of Israel.
Joel 3:16

The LORD will *roar* from on high,
and from his holy habitation *utter his voice*;
he will *roar mightily* against his fold,
and *shout*, like those who tread the grapes,
against all the inhabitants of the earth.
The *clamour* will resound to the ends of the earth,
for the LORD has an indictment against the nations;
he is entering into judgement with all flesh,
and the wicked he will put to the sword.
Jeremiah 25:30-31

The LORD *roars* from Zion,
and *utters his voice* from Jerusalem;
the pastures of the shepherds mourn,
and the top of Carmel withers.
Amos 1:2

God is in her midst [= in Jerusalem]:
she shall not be moved;
God will help her when the morning dawns.
The nations rage, the kingdoms totter.

He utters his voice and *the earth melts.*
The LORD of hosts is with us;
the God of Jacob is our refuge.

Psalm 46: 5-7

In the Book of Revelation the angel, announcing the days of the final trumpet, calls out "with a loud voice" (Revelation 10:3) and in 1 Thessalonians 4:16 "the Lord himself will descend from heaven with a cry of command" and usher in the final days.

Prayers are often described as loud cries in the Bible (Ezekiel 11:13, Nehemiah 9:4, Luke 17:15 and Revelation 6:10 are good examples) and there is little reason to suppose that Jesus did not utter a prayer as he died. But the Gospel-makers are more concerned with establishing that the moment of Jesus' death is a defining time. It marks the defeat of evil, of Satan, and the incursion of God's benign judgement on humanity. It ushers in the reign of God and announces that God's roar from Jerusalem is a trumpet blast of assurance, an assurance that God's love is finally in the world for all to see.

Thus even such a simple phrase as the "loud cry" of Jesus must not be taken at its face value, as if it were simply the casual remark of a passing journalist. An historian may have heard the final cry of Jesus but it is the Gospel-writer who interprets the deeper resonances of the divine voice.

The conclusion to be drawn from all this is that the reader of the stories of the death of Jesus must be alert to the intriguing webs of interpretation woven by Matthew, Mark, Luke and John. Every noun, verb, adjective and adverb must be scrutinised, for these grammatical building blocks are the stuff from which Gospel-makers build their houses of interpretation on the foundation stones of history. Of course, once the house is built, it is often quite difficult to find the foundation stone.

DISCUSSION SUGGESTIONS

1. Does it matter that it is exceedingly difficult, if not impossible, to separate history from interpretation? Can we, whether historians or theologians, ever separate what happened from our understanding of the meaning of what happened? Can we ever separate Jesus from the faith he inspired in his disciples?

2. Why, do you think, St Paul says that when we come together for The Eucharist we are "proclaiming the *death* of the Lord until he comes (1 Corinthians 11:26)? Why not the resurrection? Why not the death and resurrection?

3. Of all the people standing near or afar off as Jesus died, with whom would you have stood on that dark day? And why?

THE TWELFTH STATION

Jesus Dies on the Cross

ENTRANCE:

Processional music or appropriate hymn.
Unveiling of the Cross.
Lighting of candles, use of incense, or other appropriate acts of veneration of the Cross.

OPENING PRAYER RECITED BY ALL:

Almighty God,
be mindful,
we pray you,
of this your family,
for whose sake our Lord Jesus Christ,
when he was betrayed,
did not hesitate to undergo the agony of the Cross.
May our prayerful following in his footsteps
renew in us
our work of faith,
our labour of love,
and our steadfastness of hope.

RESPONSE:

We adore you, O Christ, and we praise you,
because by your holy Cross you have
redeemed the world.

A READING FROM THE GOSPEL OF ST MARK
Mark 15:16-37

Narrator 1:

The soldiers led him away inside the palace (that is, the praetorium); and they called together the whole battalion. And they clothed him in a purple cloak, and plaiting a crown of thorns they put it on him. And they began to salute him, "Hail, King of the Jews!" And they struck his head with a reed, and spat upon him, and they knelt down in homage to him. And when they had mocked him, they stripped him of the purple cloak, and put his own clothes on him. And they led him out to crucify him.

SILENT REFLECTION

Narrator 2:

They led him out to crucify him. And they compelled a passer-by, Simon of Cyrene, who was coming in from the country, the father of Alexander and Rufus, to carry his cross. And they brought him to the place called Golgotha (which means The Place of the Skull). And they offered him wine mingled with myrrh; but he did not drink it. And they crucified him, and divided his garments among them, casting lots for them, to decide what each should take.

SILENT REFLECTION

Narrator 3:

It was the third hour when they crucified him. And the inscription of the charge against him read, "The King of the Jews". And with him they crucified two robbers, one on his right and one on his left. And those who passed by derided him, wagging their heads, and saying, "Aha! You would destroy the temple and build it in three days, save yourself, and come down from the cross!" So also the chief priests mocked him to one another with the scribes, saying, "He saved others; he cannot save himself. Let the Messiah, the King of Israel, come down now from the cross, that we may see and believe." Those who were crucified with him also reviled him. When the sixth hour had come, there was darkness over the whole earth until the ninth hour. And at the ninth hour Jesus cried with a loud voice, "*E'loi, E'loi, la'ma sabach-tha-ni?*", which means, "My God, my God, why have you forsaken me?" And some of the bystanders hearing it said, "Behold, he is calling on Elijah." And one ran and, filling a sponge full of vinegar, put it on a reed and gave it to him to drink, saying, "Wait, let us see whether Elijah will come to take him down". And Jesus uttered a loud cry, and breathed his last.

ALL KNEEL IN SILENT REFLECTION

A MEDITATION

LEADER:

For the word of the cross is folly to those who
are perishing,
but to us who are being saved it is the power of
God.
For it is written,
"I will destroy the wisdom of the wise,
and the cleverness of the clever, I will thwart."
Where is the wise man?
Where is the scribe?
Where is the debater of this age?
Has not God made foolish the wisdom of this world?

1 Corinthians 1:18-20.

PEOPLE: [sung]   *O Christe Domine Jesu,*
O Christe Domine Jesu!
O Christe Domine Jesu,
O Christe Domine Jesu!

Taizé chant

LEADER: We preach Christ crucified...
Christ the power of God
and the wisdom of God.
For the foolishness of God
is wiser than human wisdom,
and the weakness of God
is stronger than human strength.

1 Corinthians 1:23-25.

PEOPLE:　　　　*O Christe Domine Jesu,*
　　　　　　　O Christe Domine Jesu!
　　　　　　　O Christe Domine Jesu,
　　　　　　　O Christe Domine Jesu!

LEADER:

We impart a secret and hidden wisdom from God,
which God decreed before the ages for our
glorification.
None of the rulers of this age understood this,
for if they had,
they would not have crucified the Lord of glory.
But it is written,
"No eye has seen,
nor ear heard,
nor the heart of man conceived,
what God has prepared for those who love him."

1 Corinthians 2:7-9

PEOPLE:　　　　*O Christe Domine Jesu,*
　　　　　　　O Christe Domine Jesu!
　　　　　　　O Christe Domine Jesu,
　　　　　　　O Christe Domine Jesu!

LEADER:

[Christ] is not weak in dealing with you,
but is powerful in you.
For he was crucified in weakness,
but lives by the power of God.

2 Corinthians 13:3-4

PEOPLE: *O Christe Domine Jesu,*
            O Christe Domine Jesu!
            O Christe Domine Jesu,
            O Christe Domine Jesu!

LEADER: Far be it from me to glory
            except in the cross of our Lord Jesus Christ,
            by which the world has been crucified to me,
            and I to the world.
            Galatians 6:14

PEOPLE: *O Christe Domine Jesu,*
            O Christe Domine Jesu!
            O Christe Domine Jesu,
            O Christe Domine Jesu!

LEADER: I have been crucified with Christ;
            it is no longer I who live,
            but Christ who lives in me;
            and the life I now live in the flesh
            I live by faith in the Son of God,
            who loved me
            and gave himself up for me.
            Galatians 2:20

PEOPLE: *O Christe Domine Jesu,*
            O Christe Domine Jesu!
            O Christe Domine Jesu,
            O Christe Domine Jesu!

LEADER:

For if we have been united with him
in a death like his,
we shall certainly be united with him
in a resurrection like his.
We know that our old self was crucified with him
so that the sinful body might be destroyed,
and we might no longer be enslaved to sin.
For he who has died is freed from sin.
But if we have died with Christ,
we believe that we shall also live with him.

Romans 6:5-8

PEOPLE:

O Christe Domine Jesu,
O Christe Domine Jesu!
O Christe Domine Jesu,
O Christe Domine Jesu!

PRAYERS OF INTERCESSION

LEADER: God so loved us that He gave his Son
to *carry* our sins,
to *bear* the intolerable burdens we place upon ourselves,
to *raise* us out of the terrors we create in our world.
Surely he has borne our griefs
and carried our sorrows.
Let us pray, therefore, with confidence
that our hearts may be open to the gospel of the
Cross of Jesus.

1. As we follow in the footsteps of Jesus,
let us pray
that our hearts may be opened to the depth and riches
and wisdom of God's love for all peoples.

ALL: Lord, in your mercy, hear our prayer.

2. As we follow in the footsteps of Jesus,
let us pray
that we rejoice in hope,
be patient in tribulation,
and constant in prayer.

ALL: Lord, in your mercy, hear our prayer.

3. As we follow in the footsteps of Jesus,
let us pray
that we bless those who deride us,
rejoice with those who rejoice,
weep with those who weep.

ALL: Lord, in your mercy, hear our prayer.

4. As we follow in the footsteps of Jesus,
let us pray that we repay no one evil for evil,
but take thought for what is good;
that we live in harmony with one another
and in peace with all people.

ALL: Lord, in your mercy, hear our prayer.

5. Bidding Prayers from the congregation.

ALL: Almighty God,
be mindful,
we pray you,
of this your family,
for whose sake our Lord Jesus Christ,
when he was betrayed,
did not hesitate to undergo the agony of the Cross.
May our prayerful following in his footsteps
renew in us
our work of faith,
our labour of love,
and our steadfastness of hope.
AMEN.

BLESSING:

May the God of steadfastness and encouragement
grant us to live in such harmony with one another,
in accord with Jesus Christ, that together we may
with one voice glorify the God and Father of our
Lord Jesus Christ.

And may the blessing of Almighty God,
Father, Son, and Holy Spirit,
come down upon us,
and remain in our hearts and in our homes forever.
AMEN.

ALL: We adore you, O Christ, and we praise you,
because by your holy Cross you have
redeemed the world.

The Cross is not covered.
All reverence/kiss the Cross and depart in silence.

Jesus is Taken Down from the Cross
and
Laid in the Tomb

BACKGROUND:

The Franciscan friars, as they celebrated Mass in Santa Croce in Florence, had before them an altarpiece by Ugolino di Nerio (d. 1339) which depicts six haloed figures, three men and three women, embracing the body of Jesus as they take it down from the cross. It is a picture which intertwines the *passion* of Jesus and the *compassion* of his mother and the other grieving disciples. The removal of the body of Jesus from the cross is not described in any detail in the Gospels, which record simply that the body was removed, wrapped in a linen shroud, and laid in a tomb. Yet by the mid-fifteenth century, through the influence of Giotto's *Lamentation* (Arena Chapel, Padua) and such hymns as Jacopone da Todi's *Stabat Mater*, the *Addolorata*, the image of the grieving mother cradling her dead son, had become a standard image in art and devotional literature. In the early fifteenth century, St Bernadino of Siena wrote of Mary holding her dead Son as she had held him at his birth, "believing that the days of Bethlehem had returned... and that he was sleeping, and she cradled him to her breast. She imagined the winding sheet in which he was wrapped to be his swaddling clothes". The most startling of images of the deposition is the Donatello bronze relief in the Victoria and Albert Museum (London). The movement towards realism in art and sensibility in literature and piety both promote and reflect Christian understanding of Mary, the mother of Jesus.

In contrast to this outpouring of artistic genius and concomitant piety, the first three Gospels, Mark, Matthew and Luke, state simply that the body of Jesus was quickly disposed of, with no lamentation and no honourable burial rites (John's Gospel is significantly different). An honourable Jewish burial, such as we know from sources somewhat later than the first century, would have involved washing the corpse, anointing it with oil, laying it out, binding up the chin, closing the eyes, trimming the hair, covering the head with a veil, clothing the body with care, and binding the hands and feet.

Concerning incidents leading to the Jewish War (66-73 AD), one reporter who fought in that war, Josephus, the historian, condemns Idumeans for failing to bury Jews they had slaughtered: "they proceeded to that degree of impiety, as to cast away their dead bodies without burial, although the Jews used to take so much care of the burial of men that they took down those who had been condemned and crucified, and buried them before the going down of the sun" (*Jewish War*, 4.5.2.317). The Book of Deuteronomy states: "If a man has committed a crime punishable by death and he is put to death, and you hang him on a tree [= crucifixion], his body shall not remain all night on the tree, but you shall bury him the same day, for a hanged man is accursed by God" (Deuteronomy 21:22-23). But Josephus interprets these words of the *Torah* as follows: "He that blasphemes God, let him be stoned, and let him hang upon a tree all that day, and then let him be buried in an ignominious and obscure manner" (Antiquities, 4.8.6.202). Burial, yes. Dignity, no.

Yet the Roman practice was to deprive executed criminals of the rite of burial and to leave them to rot and be scavenged by carrion birds and wild dogs. Was the body of Jesus abandoned to scavengers or was it buried? And, if it was buried, was it a hasty disposal of a crucified criminal or an honourable internment?

From a Jewish point of view, there are two indications that Jesus would have been buried. First, condemned by priestly authority as a blasphemer, Jesus died as the Feast of Passover was about to be celebrated (whether Jesus died on the eve or the first day of the feast is much debated) and, it would seem, as the Sabbath approached. Jewish sensitivity would demand that neither the Passover nor the Sabbath be profaned by a naked crucified corpse remaining in public view. Secondly, the demands of the *Torah*, as expressed in Deuteronomy, required immediate burial, if not an honourable one.

From a Roman point of view, Jesus had been condemned to death, not by Jewish authorities but by Pilate, the prefect who, in the exercise of his duty, sent Jesus to death as one claiming to be King of the

Jews. Is it likely, knowing what we know of Pilate, knowing what we know of his boss, the emperor Tiberius (see John 19:12 for the *real politique*), and the almost total absence of any archaeological remains of any of the hundreds of thousands of crucifixion's victims, that Jesus was an exception to what was everywhere else the rule?

The discovery of the bones of the crucified Yehohanan (see Background to the Eleventh Station) provides two pieces of evidence that are supportive of the Gospel contention that Pilate handed over the body of Jesus to Joseph of Arimathea. First, there is the fact that we now know of an exception to the almost universal rule that crucified corpses were deliberately withheld from family and friends and left to rot. Secondly, Yehohanan was buried in a complex burial area in a rock-hewn tomb. In other words, his family had money and money talks.

Joseph of Arimathea was a member of the Jewish council and was able to gain access to Pilate. He "took courage", so Mark tells us, indicating that his request was entirely beyond what was normally permitted and was, indeed, contrary to state policy. He was able to provide a tomb which had been hewn out of a rock and was sealed by a rolled stone, a tomb, that is, of a wealthy family. It is possible that Joseph was able to secure for Jesus what the family of Yehohanan had secured for that unfortunate young man. It is noticeable that the family and disciples of Jesus were not involved in securing or burying the body of Jesus.

DISCUSSION SUGGESTIONS

Great artists have interpreted many moments from the Gospels, from the Annunciation to Mary to the Resurrection of Jesus. The writings of St Bernard of Clairvaux (1090-1153) and the religious renewal brought about by the followers of St Francis emphasised devotion to the Passion of Jesus and inspired an outburst of artistic endeavour. *The Deposition* by Ugolino di Nerio (c.1317), the *Lamentation of the Virgin Mary over the Dead Christ*, a sculpture by Donatello (c.1455), and *Saint Francis Embracing the Crucified Christ* by the Spaniard, Francisco Ribalta (c.1620), might inspire quiet contemplation and prayer in keeping with the solemn silence which Holy Saturday demands.

Jesus is Taken Down from the Cross
and
Laid in the Tomb

ENTRANCE:

Act of reverence to the uncovered Cross.

HYMN: *When I survey the wondrous cross…*
Isaac Watts (1674-1748)

OPENING PRAYER RECITED BY ALL:

Almighty God,
be mindful,
we pray you,
of this your family,
for whose sake our Lord Jesus Christ,
when he was betrayed,
did not hesitate to undergo the agony of the Cross.
May our prayerful following in his footsteps
renew in us
our work of faith,
our labour of love,
and our steadfastness of hope.

RESPONSE:

We adore you, O Christ, and we praise you,
because by your holy Cross you have
redeemed the world.

A READING FROM THE GOSPEL OF ST MARK
Mark 15:42-47

READER:
When evening had come, since it was the Day of
Preparation, that is, the day before the Sabbath, Joseph
of Arimathea, a respected member of the council,
who was also himself looking for the kingdom of
God, took courage and went to Pilate, and asked for
the body of Jesus. And Pilate wondered if he were
already dead; and summoning the centurion, he asked
him if he were already dead. And when he learned
from the centurion that he was already dead, he
granted the body to Joseph. And he bought a linen
shroud, and taking him down, wrapped him in the
linen shroud, and laid him in a tomb which had been
hewn out of the rock; and he rolled a stone against
the door of the tomb. Mary Magdalene and Mary the
mother of Joses saw where he was laid.

SILENT REFLECTION

HYMN: *O sacred head sore wounded ...*
                  Paulus Gerhardt (1607-76)

A READING FROM THE BOOK OF DANIEL
Daniel 12:1-3

READER:

At that time shall arise Michael, the great prince who has charge of your people. And there shall be a time of trouble, such as never has been since there was a nation till that time; but at that time your people shall be delivered, every one whose name shall be found written in the book. And many of those who sleep in the dust of the earth shall awake, some to everlasting life, and some to shame and everlasting contempt. And those who are wise shall shine like the brightness of the firmament; and those who turn many to righteousness, like the stars forever and ever.

SILENT REFLECTION

Watching…

READER/CANTOR: O LORD,
                   how many are my foes!
            Many are rising against me;
              many are saying of me,
          there is no help for him in God.
                   Psalm 3:1–2

ALL: [sung]   *Kyrie, eleison.*
                     Kyrie, eleison.
                     Kyrie, eleison.

READER/CANTOR:
>When I call, answer me,
>O God of my right.
>In my distress you have set me free.
>Be gracious to me,
>and hear my prayer.
>Psalm 4:1

ALL:
>*Christe, eleison.*
>*Christe, eleison.*
>*Christe, eleison.*

READER/CANTOR: O LORD,
>give ear to my words,
>give heed to my groaning.
>Listen to the sound of my cry,
>my King and my God,
>for to you do I pray.
>Psalm 5:1-2

ALL:
>*Kyrie, eleison.*
>*Kyrie, eleison.*
>*Kyrie, eleison.*

READER/CANTOR: O LORD
>turn [to me],
>save my life;
>deliver me.
>for the sake of your steadfast love.
>For in death there is no remembrance;
>who can give you praise from the grave?
>Psalm 6:4-5

ALL: *Lord, have mercy.*
                        Lord, have mercy.
                        Lord, have mercy.

READER/CANTOR: Rise up,
                        O LORD
                   in your anger;
          lift yourself up against the fury of my enemies.
                        Awake,
                        O my God,
                   you have appointed a judgement.
                   Let the assembly of the peoples
                        be gathered around you...
                   The LORD judges the peoples.
                        Judge me,
                        O LORD,
                   according to my righteousness,
               and according to the integrity that is in me.
                        Psalm 7:6-8

ALL: *Christ, have mercy.*
                        Christ, have mercy.
                        Christ, have mercy.

READER/CANTOR:

          The LORD is a stronghold for the oppressed,
                   a stronghold in times of trouble.
          And those who know your name put their trust
                        in you.
                        O LORD,
          you have not forsaken those who seek you...

For the needy shall not always be forgotten,
and the hope of the poor shall not perish forever.

Psalm 9:9-10 and 18.

All: *Lord, have mercy.*
                        Lord, have mercy.
                        Lord, have mercy.

READER/CANTOR: O LORD,
                        how long?
            Will you forget me forever?
        How long will you hide your face from me?
            How long must I bear pain in my soul,
        and have sorrow in my heart all the long day?
        How long shall my enemy be exalted over me?
                Consider and answer me,
                    O LORD my God;
                    lighten my eyes,
            lest I sleep the sleep of death.

Psalm 13:1-3

ALL: *Kyrie, eleison.*
                        Kyrie, eleison.
                        Kyrie, eleison.

READER/CANTOR: My God!
                        My God!
            Why have you forsaken me?
        Why are you so far from helping me,
        so far from the words of my sorrow?
                O my God,

I cry by day,
but you do not answer,
by night,
but find no peace!
Psalm 22:1-2

ALL:
Christe, eleison.
Christe, eleison.
Christe, eleison.

READER/CANTOR:

I am poured out like water,
and all my bones are out of joint;
my heart is like wax,
it is melted within my breast;
my strength is dried up like a potsherd,
and my tongue sticks to my jaws;
you lay me in the dust of death.
Yes, dogs are round about me;
a company of evildoers encircle me;
they have pierced my hands and feet –
I can count my bones! –
they stare and gloat over me;
they divide my garments among them,
and for my clothing they cast lots.
My God!
My God!
Why have you forsaken me?
Psalm 22:14-19

ALL: *Kyrie, eleison.*
                        Kyrie, eleison.
                        Kyrie, eleison.

PRAYERS OF INTERCESSION

LEADER: God so loved us that He gave his Son
to *carry* our sins,
to *bear* the intolerable burdens we place upon ourselves,
to *raise* us out of the terrors we create in our world.
Surely he has borne our griefs
and carried our sorrows.
Let us pray, therefore, with confidence that our hearts
may be open to the gospel of the Cross of Jesus.

1. As we follow in the footsteps of Jesus,
let us pray
that our hearts may be opened to the depth and riches
and wisdom of God's love for all peoples.

ALL: Lord, in your mercy, hear our prayer.

2. As we follow in the footsteps of Jesus,
let us pray
that we rejoice in hope,
be patient in tribulation,
and constant in prayer.

ALL: Lord, in your mercy, hear our prayer.

3. As we follow in the footsteps of Jesus,
let us pray
that we bless those who deride us,

rejoice with those who rejoice,
weep with those who weep.

ALL: Lord, in your mercy, hear our prayer.

4. As we follow in the footsteps of Jesus,
let us pray
for those who have gone before us
that they may be safe in God's heart.

ALL: Eternal rest grant unto them, O Lord,
and may perpetual light shine upon them.
May they rest in peace.
And may their souls
and the souls of all the departed,
through the mercy of God,
rest in peace. AMEN.

ALL: Almighty God,
                       be mindful,
                      we pray you,
                    of this your family,
            for whose sake our Lord Jesus Christ,
                   when he was betrayed,
      did not hesitate to undergo the agony of the Cross.
          May our prayerful following in his footsteps
                        renew in us
                      our work of faith,
                     our labour of love,
                and our steadfastness of hope.
                           AMEN.

May the God of steadfastness and encouragement
grant us to live in such harmony with one another,
in accord with Jesus Christ, that together we may
with one voice glorify the God and Father of our
Lord Jesus Christ.

And may the blessing of Almighty God,
Father, Son, and Holy Spirit,
come down upon us,
and remain in our hearts and in our homes forever.

AMEN.

ALL: We adore you, O Christ, and praise you,
        because by your holy Cross you have
            redeemed the world.

All reverence/kiss the Cross and depart in silence.